D1521000

The Maul:
Preparing for the Chaos
of Close Combatives

Schalk Holloway and Gavin Coleman

I could easily just state that this is one of the best books on knife combatives I have read, ever, and be done with it, but that would be a disservice to both the authors and to you, the reader. This is a book that covers the actual whys, delving into brain models, behavior, accessing mind states for training. In short, it lays out the most important aspect of training the human animal. The authors go science heavy without being boring, and always hook it back in to the subject at hand. And then you get to the meat of the matter...The Maul. It is, quite simply, the best approach to realistic knife combatives written in years. It is not a collection of techniques; it is not a flip book of photos. It does not boast of being unbeatable. It lays out an effective way of using the pikal grip in a combative situation. The whys of the grip, the how's, and the necessary attributes to employ it. And, as a bonus, it has a training method to get you up to speed rapidly and relatively safe. I cannot give it a higher recommendation than this, read it, practice it, read it again, and keep working it. This is good stuff. I wish this book was out when I started in this arena.

Terry Trahan – Instructor, Masters of Mayhem

Reading 'The Maul' as a review for Schalk and Gavin was a sheer pleasure. As I read it, I saw thoughts crystallize into reality. There is far too much drivel and nonsense in the martial arts/combatives/self defense world/s. To actually read a really well researched, evidence based and thoroughly tested piece of work like this is real pleasure. Drawing on the work of Marc MacYoung and Rory Miller provides a very sound foundation, the scientific research presented builds on that foundation and the whole package is presented in a way that is easily digestible and can be adapted into your training rapidly. I taught some of the content on the night I finished reviewing the book, yes, it is that good, and my students, instructor and senior instructor who were present clearly benefited from it, as did I. The Maul is recommended reading for anyone serious about self-improvement and advancing their knowledge, I train Ju Jitsu (traditional with a modern edge) and self-defense (not the same things at all), and I can see lots of ways that 'The Maul' can improve how we train and inform why we train. As I said earlier, we used it last night. Maybe we have the honor of being the 1st.

Garry Smith – Editor, Conflict Manager Magazine / Chief Instructor, The Academy of Self Defense

CONTENTS

INTRODUCTION

ON THE PURPOSE OF THIS BOOK

The knowledge contained in this book originated as a response to certain doubts, doubts that were surfacing from trying to apply certain learned close combat methods to actual critical and/or close combat incidents. These doubts led to questions, and unfortunately, even though the authors of this book have actually trained quite deeply in existing close combat systems, these questions were not being adequately answered by these existing systems. The primary driving factors of these doubts, listed with their corresponding questions, related to the following three very closely interrelated issues:

- There was a clear degradation in performance and execution under certain conditions. The question was whether we could identify these conditions above and beyond ways which were already proposed, as, if these existing ways obviously aren't solving the problem, we should be asking ourselves what we're missing.
- Existing techniques, tactics and procedures would lose effectiveness once attempted in an extremely chaotic environment. The main question here was why? What are the elements in the chaotic environment that cause this loss of effectiveness? Precisely why does the operator struggle under these conditions? And what are the elements in existing training methodologies that fail to prepare us correctly?
- Long time students and trainees, who were not regularly exposed to violence, initially fail to adapt their training to the actual close combat environment. First of all, we just want to say that we have no problem with any individual that is training for but has never experienced violence. If you are not operating in a field in which you purposefully have to engage with violence there is no reason for you to go looking for it. Unfortunately the industry is now filled with wannabe operators, and these days it seems wannabe gangsters, that look down on those who want to avoid violence. This is stupid and shouldn't even be regarded. That said, the question remains: Why does someone train for a very long time but the training doesn't translate to high efficacy and success in an actual incident?

These doubts and corresponding questions first and foremost forced us to look beyond the idea of learning a specific martial art or close combat system. What we found was that these problems, essentially, were all problems of the brain. They are breakdowns in the brain's ability to recognise, adapt and respond adequately under certain conditions. An elbow is an elbow; irrespective of which martial arts or close combat system it comes from. But the inability to accurately judge when and how to use said elbow, as well as the inability to correctly execute the elbow in line with that judgment whilst in the chaos of an actual close combat incident, these are issues of the brain.

This book then is an exploration into what relevant knowledge we can take from the most recent brain research regarding this breakdown, and how we can apply that knowledge into better training methodologies for close combat incidents.

WHAT CAN BE EXPECTED

Depth of knowledge: There will be something in this book for everyone interested in the topic. Whether operator, instructor or training enthusiast, the knowledge base is deep enough that you will be able to learn and apply various principles and methods regardless of your background or context.

A non systemic approach in Parts 1 - 3 and an integrative approach in Part 4: We purposefully did not want to provide the readers with just another close combat system. We wanted the readers, who might come from any background, to be able to integrate the knowledge into their existing training or operational methods. It was important though to display HOW to practically do so. As such, Part 4 contains much of The Maul, the edge and point system developed in response to the doubts and questions listed above, as well as their resulting findings. These methods are currently used in all of our training that we provide and the results are speaking for themselves.

The knowledge base for a complete edge and point system for those that need one: Part 4 contains enough of a base that anyone, regardless of their context or background, can immediately start training in The Maul. We want to be realistic though about the fact that learning close combat from written media isn't necessarily the most sensible approach. But if you do know what you are doing you'll be able to systematize it fast and well. That said though, we have decided to start a video based media channel to assist those that are serious about training in the system. You can connect with the authors directly should you be interested.

A discussion on combative knives: Gavin Coleman, the owner and artisan of Ironside Edgeworks, is quickly rising to become one of the most prominent custom knife and tool makers for the close combat environment. Apart from fully co-authoring the rest of the book he has provided a complete chapter discussing the combative knife. If you as reader do not come from an edge and pointed weapon use background, we would recommend that you read this chapter before dealing into the rest of Part 4.

FINAL INTRODUCTORY WORDS

In the Glossary you will find words and terms used specifically and frequently throughout the book. If you find a word or term capitalized anywhere in the book it means you can refer back to it in the Glossary. The Glossary will provide just enough concise information so that you can fix and refresh the meaning and use of the word of term.

The themes in Part 1 of the book, like some of the rest of book, actually contain an incredible depth of knowledge. However, one of the challenges in writing this book was to consider how much to add when it came to related or intersecting fields of study. We did feel it necessary to concisely develop the theme of violence. We also wanted to base this development primarily on the works that we originally built our own foundational understanding on. However, in the attempt to keep those chapters concise, and to retain the actual focus of the book, we have done so at the risk of lack of depth. The purpose of those chapters is purely to prime readers who are completely new to the topics of violence for the rest of the book. If there are any shortcomings in this section of the book we claim full responsibility. Please make the time to study the works of the authors cited there.

You will notice that there is a very large focus on movement in the book. This is because all techniques and procedures are, at their most fundamental levels, simply movement patterns. The brain can classify and recall a movement pattern as a technique or a procedure, but it executes a movement. We want to encourage you to start adapting to this way of thought as it will assist you tremendously throughout your reading. Finally, always remember that we attempted to find the sweet spot between deep knowledge and wide application. There is much more to learn on these topics. Where relevant we have suggested further reading material. You would do well to read more, but, the real growth will be in applying what you learn to your training and operational methods. We want to encourage you to do the work of thinking through and actually integrating what you learn.

One of the authors of this book has trained high level tactical response team instructors, park rangers, mountain guides, security specialists, law enforcement agents working in spheres ranging from the liquor authority to South Africa's version of federal law enforcement, to regular civilians and training enthusiasts. Apart from this background as instructor he has personally operated within civilian, security and law enforcement environments as operator and as team leader and has more than 15 years hands on experience in the resolution of various forms of violent encounters. These methods were born from, and developed within, the context of actual close combat incidents. They work and they can confidently be incorporated into whatever methods you are already practicing. But you will need to do the work of understanding and applying it.

Our trust is that this book will shape your perception on training and that it will tremendously increase your performance in chaos. Enjoy it and stay safe.

PART ONE – THE CONTEXT OF VIOLENCE

CHAPTER 1: PURPOSE OF VIOLENCE

DEFINITIONS OF VIOLENCE

As our country, South Africa, is frequently confirmed as one of the more violent societies in the world, we have had numerous studies done on how it came to be so. One such study, done by the Centre for the Study of Violence and Reconciliation (CSVR) and commissioned by our Department: Safety and Security, titled "The Violent Nature of Crime in South Africa" was released in June 2007. In this report a working definition for violence was penned down:

Applications, or threats, of physical force against a person, which can give rise to criminal or civil liability, whether severe or not and whether with or without a weapon

We don't fully agree with this definition. This definition was formulated specifically within the context of violent crime, and as such we understand how it developed as it is. However, as a definition for violence holistically it is lacking, and here are three reasons why:

1. **It excludes the purpose of violence from the definition.**

    1.1. Violence is always about getting something. If person A is becoming violent with person B there has to be some form of motivation for it. Regardless of whether the motivation is deemed valid, rational, internal or externally motivated, there is still some form of motivation present. Meaning person A is trying to achieve something.

    1.2. The reason person A is considering, threatening or using force, is because person B does not want to acquiesce to person A's agenda. Or in straight forward English – person B does not want to give person A what he wants. In this sense the threat or use of force is purposed to coerce person B into compliance.

    1.3. This is the essential purpose of violence. To get something that another person does not want to give.

3

2. It assumes all violence is physical by mechanism of execution.

    2.1. As we start to understand this purpose of violence – and we delve deeper into it much more as we progress through this chapter – it should become obvious that physical force is not the only way to coerce compliance. Think about disciplinary processes in a workplace environment. A disciplinary process is intended to force or ensure some form of behavior in the workplace. A disciplinary process resulting in suspension or termination of services is essentially a threat of financial violence.

    2.2. If you consider a heated and out of control argument between a married couple, we can frequently see a form of verbal or emotional violence taking place. The husband may say hurtful or critical things to the wife as he attempts to "win" the argument. The wife might do the same possibly trying to manipulate the husband into complying with her agenda.

    2.3. It is important to remember that there are many ways to be violent. Not just physical. Frequently individuals or groups that shy away from physical violence are very violent in other ways. They just don't like or are afraid of physical violence.

3. It excludes the possibility of violence as a positive contributor.

    3.1. This point is a much contested issue in many of today's societies. The purpose of this book however is not to get involved in any philosophical or political posturing, but rather to speak about and to current reality. As such we need to remember the following: If the day comes that you or others are physically and relentlessly attacked or assaulted, the probability is very high that only a forceful or violent response will repel such an attack. If your back is against the wall and an arm is coming at you with a stab, and another stab, and another stab and another, in that moment, the effective use of force is the singular activity that will save your life. If a murderer is loose in your school or in your shopping centre shooting and stabbing as many children and adults as they can, the effective use of force is the singular activity that will stop them in that moment.

3.2. I agree with the fact that there are other options on strategic, diplomatic, socio-economical and interpersonal relational levels with which we can attempt to resolve future acts of violence. And I honestly believe we should pursue long term peace and joy on all levels, but right there in the moment, when someone is attempting to take your life or the life of another innocent person, you will either use some form of force or they will achieve what they have set out to do.

For these three reasons we define violence in the following way:

Applications, or threats, of any type of force (verbal, physical, sexual, financial, emotional, psychological or social) against a person or persons, with the aim of coercing some form of compliance.

TYPES OF VIOLENCE

Holding this definition of violence in mind, have a look at the diagram below:

Peyton Quin	Territorial Violence	Behavior Correcting					
Marc MacYoung's Kinds of Violence	Territorial Violence	Behavior Correcting			Criminal Violence		Predatory Violence
Schalk Holloway	Territorial Violence	Behavior Changing			Criminal Violence	Egocentric Violence	Predatory Violence
Rory Millers Types of Violence	Territory Defense	Educational Beatdown	Monkey Dance (incl. Group)	Status Seeking Show	Resource Predator		Process Predator
Rory Miller's Two Categories	**Social Violence**				**A-Social Violence**		

For the purpose of this discussion we will primarily focus on Marc MacYoung's Kinds of Violence model. His model offers very simple and clear insight into the purpose and possible peaceful resolution of the potentially violent situation. We will briefly touch on Rory Miller's two categories, to help us better understand some of Marc's model. We are honorably mentioning Peyton Quinn's model, this is where Marc MacYoung started and developed his model from. We have added one more type of violence to Marc MacYoung's model and have also slightly changed the naming of one of the types. We will discuss why we have done so when we get there.

Lastly, kindly note that we are not aware of Marc MacYoung or Rory Miller typing their models together in this way. Their models actually have different nuances and focuses. We have however placed them like this as we do feel elements can be likened to each other when attempting to gain a broad overview on the topic, and as stated in the introduction, it might provide the reader who has no insight into the topic a firm foundation.

All of that said, the primary reason we would like to understand the types of violence is simple: In understanding the types we can understand why a person is considering the use of force; understanding which type of violence we're dealing with gives us insight into what the potentially violent or violent person wants. When we have a clear understanding of what this person wants we also gain insight into other ways of resolving the situation, possibly without the use of force. Furthermore, by understanding what this person wants we can also make better decisions relating to our own use of force, specifically whether it's necessary and how much force to apply.

TERRITORIAL VIOLENCE

What does the violent person want? He wants you to leave.

Peaceful resolution: Leave.

Territorial violence, although very simple in purpose, can feature in a variety of circumstances. Due to its territorial nature it very frequently pertains to some form of tribalism or localism. We can find it on a strategic level between nations, when border regulations are ignored or with certain types of displays of force or capabilities. In societal structures we can find it in gang or drug infested areas, we can also find it in activities or locations that foster a sense of local ownership (like surfers at a local beach or regulars at a bar).

It is also a natural phenomenon in any situation where a person or persons is trying to protect their territory. A home owner trying to protect their possessions or family might threaten or commit territorial violence if the transgressor does not leave. Rory Miller calls this type territory defense.

BEHAVIOR CHANGING VIOLENCE

What does the violent person want? He wants you to change what you are doing.

Peaceful resolution: Change your behavior.

Marc MacYoung calls this type behavior correcting violence. He does so primarily because he is speaking from the viewpoint of the violent person. The violent person is threatening or using force to align the other person's behavior

7

with what they deem to be correct. It is arguable though whether from another point of view the new expectation on the behavior would objectively be correct. For this reason we rather call it Behavior Changing Violence.

As related earlier, workplace discipline can fall into this type. Demands on a person to stop acting in a certain way or to stop communicating in a certain way, coupled with some form of consequential punishment (think disciplining a child or a domestically violent response to a spouse shouting at their significant other), are forms of behavior changing violence. Although we won't go into it, Rory Miller's educational beat downs frequently fall into this sphere. Simply put, the moment coercive demands and consequences are set around specific behaviors ie. "If you don't stop this or do this then I or we WILL" we are dealing with behavior changing violence. In this sense most of the other types are actually forms of behavior changing violence but still merit their own insight.

CRIMINAL VIOLENCE

What does the violent person want? He wants something that is yours.

Peaceful resolution: Give him what he wants.

Criminal violence in its purest form is for profit. Acts are perpetrated purely for economic gain. Whether it's burglarizing a house or robbing a convenience store or an unsuspecting pedestrian, the purpose of the violence is to acquire something for economic gain. Rory Miller calls these perpetrators resource predators as they are attacking others for resources. It is a very simple type of violence to understand.

Sometimes the attacker will give you prior warning, meaning they will give you the option to comply with their demands. Sometimes they will just attack you and attempt to take what they want. However, when we are dealing purely with criminal violence, and the option is given to you to comply, the chances are really good that you will not be attacked if you do comply.

EGOCENTRIC VIOLENCE

What does the violent person want? He wants to feel dominant.

Peaceful resolution: None guaranteed, attempt to boost ego.

This is the type that we have added to the list. It relates to any situation where the potentially violent person is attempting to feed an egocentric need. It is closely interrelated with predatory violence. The reason we split it from predatory violence is because you are sometimes able to peacefully resolve this type whereas with predatory violence you are not. Rory Miller's monkey dances and status seeking shows frequently fall into this type. Bullies fall within this and the predatory violence. Many forms of show or seeking of dominance, whether intra-tribe (between different status levels in an organization), inter-tribe (between different teams or gangs), within a family system (domestic violence or parental violence) falls into this category. It is predominantly social violence and not a-social violence as we'll discuss below.

If you are able to understand the violent person's egotistical need you can attempt to cater for it. This is no guarantee that you will be let off the hook as sometimes the violent person may have switched over to a form of predatory violence.

PREDATORY VIOLENCE

What does the violent person want? He wants to hurt you.

Peaceful resolution: None.

Predatory violence can be approached from two different viewpoints. First of all, predatory violence can be related to the person. Rory Miller types these individuals resource, process or survival predators. These are people who are comfortable predating on others to fulfill a specific need. Typically, the criminal that stabs you first and then takes your belongings could more easily be classified as a resource predator. Serial rapists, serial murderers, terrorists and so forth predominantly fall into the process predator type. In this sense of predatory violence relating to a person, we would classify it as a-social violence (see next heading).

Second, predatory violence can be related to intent. It is an incident in which an individual has crossed the line of peaceful resolution and has now determined to harm you. In this sense predatory violence could have been another type of violence that has now become predatory violence due to the target's mismanagement of the process. The essential factor here is that the violent person has now decided to hurt you and is aiming to do so. In the sense of predatory violence relating to intent, we could classify it as either social or a-social violence depending on specific incident.

Either way, when you are dealing with predatory violence you are dealing with a committed attacker and attack. There is therefore no option for peaceful resolution. The only options you have are to escape, defend or mitigate the consequences of the attack. All three of these options will be discussed in a later chapter. For now it is important to note that there is a type of violence to which there is no peaceful resolution.

RORY MILLER'S TWO CATEGORIES

We have briefly mentioned where Rory Miller's different types of violence could fit in with Marc MacYoung's model. It is of value though to touch on the two different categories of violence into which Miller's types are sorted. They are called social and a-social violence.

Social violence is violence that occurs intra-species. It is governed by the specific specie's societal constructs and norms. Humans, being a tribal species by nature, are frequently governed by the need to survive and establish dominance. For most humans there is an escalation necessary to commit social violence; most humans are not able or willing to commit violence – specifically more forceful methods of physical violence - without an initial phase in which they prepare themselves to do so. If you think about a typical bar fight, there is usually some posturing or a trade of words and insults before it becomes physical. The most frequent goal with this type of social bar fight is to establish dominance. It is not necessary, or particularly safe to either party, to try and establish dominance by immediately becoming physical as physical violence easily leads to injury and death. To increase the odds of survival, the human brain first tries to establish dominance through the use of other methods. If you are the target and you can identify what type of violence (Territorial, Behavior Changing, Egotistical) you're dealing with you can possibly resolve the situation peacefully by submitting to what the aggressor wants.

A-social violence occurs inter-species or cross species. It is what one species does and is comfortable doing to another species. It is not governed by the specie in question's societal norms or constructs. It does not come with the same deeply seated emotional ties as social violence. If you think about stepping on an ant, for most of us that creates no emotional tension whatsoever as it does not relate to the societal norms that govern our specie. There is no build up phase required to step on the ant. If we so choose we can simply step on the ant and carry on with life. Hunting is a form of a-social violence. We have a need for a resource – meat or skin – so we hunt. We might do so respectfully, but we still do so. Few humans would hunt another human for meat or skin, most humans don't have any problem hunting an animal for it. Lions don't consider the antelope when hunting.

It is important to understand these two categories. When we are faced with resource predators and process predators we are faced with a-social violence. We are faced with a predator that is NOT conforming to or functioning within the human species' societal norms. Therefore, there can be no expectation of grace or mercy when it comes to dealing with these two types of predators.

Many criminals that commit criminal violence are not pure resource or process predators. Meaning, they do not actually want to hurt you or enjoy hurting you – they actually just want your belongings. However, some criminals are pure resource or process predators. They have no issue with hurting you or killing you before, during or even after getting your belongings. They are functioning within an a-social violence category. Obviously the problem is that we never really know which we are dealing with until it is almost too late.

The moment that we deal with Marc MacYoung's predatory violence however we are dealing with a-social violence. Whether it is another type of violence that has become predatory violence, or whether it is a pure predator, we are dealing with an individual that has turned us into an object. They are approaching us as something that falls into a different species than which they do. Whether they know it or not – you have become an object to them and their intention is to damage that object.

IN SUMMARY

When it comes to dealing with violence we frequently hear one of two responses: Always submit, or, always resist. When thinking about a mugging it would mean one of the following responses: Always give your wallet. Or always fight the mugger. The reality though is that neither of these two responses will always guarantee our desired outcome.

11

Many criminal gangs actually have a mixture of pure criminals and predators. There can be four pure Criminals, that just want your wallet, and there can be one process predator hiding amongst them that wants to stab or rape you. We find this frequently in home invasions in South Africa where there are documented cases of criminals standing guard and protecting the victims from the predators in the group.

Alternatively, supposing there are just two muggers, both might be pure criminals. They just want the wallet. Great. Give it to them. Or conversely, there might just be two muggers but both of them are process predators. They want your wallet but they're going to have fun hurting you while they take it. Not so great. You'll have to fight if you want to get out of there.

And this is the essential argument of this chapter. We don't know exactly what we're dealing with until we are dealing with it. The question is not should we submit or should we fight – the question is when do we submit and when do we fight?

CHAPTER TWO – NATURE OF VIOLENCE

Before we kick off this chapter I want to introduce you to a concept we originally called "Pete-stions." It is the name Pete and the word questions that have been combined. Who was Pete? Pete was an amazing client that Schalk had the privilege of working with in 2017. He was as sharp as can be and he came from a very high level operational background. Pete's temperament though always leaned towards compartmentalizing concepts, he was a reductionist by nature and attempted to understand and assimilate knowledge through a process of identifying a concept, clearly defining its boundaries, and then filling in those boundaries with needed knowledge. You unfortunately cannot do that with the study of violence. The main problem lies with the fact that there are no clearly defined boundaries on certain of its themes. The knowledge base of certain aspects of violence strongly overlap. It is almost impossible to neatly separate all aspects into perfectly defined compartments. When it came to Pete's questions we had to create a method for determining when we should try to clearly define a concept and to neatly separate it from another, and when we should settle for a bit of overlap. Hence, the term Pete-stion was born. A Pete-stion thus is any question that tries to separate concepts like this:

When they actually look more like this:

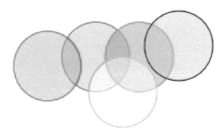

So as we start this discussion, and as we progress through this book, remember that you'll find some overlap in certain concepts and themes. This is normal. The concepts give us ways to access the study of violence. They are different entry points. If you try to completely separate all of them from each other you will most probably develop a headache. Take a moment to consider these thoughts from Rory Miller's Facing Violence: Preparing for the Unexpected:

Fights are multi-layered. The four elements: you, the Threat(s), the environment and luck; physical and mental forces; legal and social customs; what the fight is about and what both parties think it is about. The more broadly you can see the situation, the more options you have and the more dangers you can avoid. Being aware of the physical environment gives you tools and allows you to avoid hazards. Recognizing the legal limitations on force can both keep you out of trouble and possibly provide leverage ("Is this worth going to prison, son?") [Miller, Rory. Facing Violence: Preparing for the Unexpected (Kindle Locations 3010-3016). YMAA Publication Center. Kindle Edition.]

It should not take much consideration to understand that the four elements he lists will influence each other dynamically. They add many levels of complexity and they consistently create chaos, or change. More importantly, chaos which needs to be managed within extremely small windows of time (more on this later though). The purpose of this chapter is simply to help you develop an understanding and a form of respect for the Nature of Violence - especially if you have not been involved in any or many altercations.

There is a reason bombs are used in the military. They are built to be fast and accurate. They inherently remove complexity and the potential for dynamism from the equation and thus significantly increase the predictability of the outcome. It is for this same reason that the age-old "sucker punch" or the surprise assassination type stabs have remained with us throughout history.

All of that said, let's consider the following definition of the Nature of Violence:

Violence is inherently complex, extremely dynamic and therefore has an unpredictable outcome.

Let us break that down into its parts.

14

VIOLENCE IS INHERENTLY COMPLEX

Violence is, strictly speaking, chaotic but not random. There are identifiable factors that contribute to any violent incident and we can definitely attempt to understand these factors. The challenge however is twofold: One, it is difficult to understand ALL of the factors present in any given incident simply because they are not all visible or apparent. And two, it is even more difficult to understand what is going to happen when these factors start to influence each other. It is important to realise that violence, specifically as it pertains to this study, is essentially an interaction between humans. Thus, one subset of these factors pertains to the direct contributions made by each of the human role players involved in the incident. The participants of the interaction may resemble or differ from each other on any number of these factors. As such, it is both the different factors themselves, as well as how they relate to each other that add to the inherent complexity of the incident.

Let us look at three of the more accessible of these factors as both example and discussion. These three more accessible factors are background, training and motivation. Also, we will pretend we are evaluating them in the context of an argument between two men in a bar.

BACKGROUND

Both of these men have unique and separate backgrounds. What would seem to be normal or acceptable behavior to each of them differ. There are a myriad of elements that would have influenced this: Their socio economic status which in turn would have dictated the type of community they grew up in. Past experiences with violence in which they or others were possibly either injured or not. The societal code for dealing with violence and human interaction that they grew up with. The role models they had and the social groups that they hung out with and that subsequently shaped them. All of these and more will now influence their understanding of how to resolve this incident. For one it might be as simple as punching the other if he doesn't back off. For the other it might be stabbing his opponent before he can get punched. Unless we intimately know this person in front of us we have no idea what would be normal or acceptable behavior to them.

I (Schalk) have had multiple incidents in my life where I punched someone only to have them pull a firearm on me. Let that sink in for a moment. You might think it was overbearing of my opponent to do so. You may be right. But what you or I think at that moment is irrelevant. Their method for dealing with the incident was different than mine. And I could not tell that in advance.

TRAINING

The interesting dynamic about training is that it might be good or bad. Good training actually increases our odds of dealing with challenges successfully. Note the concept of odds - there are very few certainties when it comes to violence. Bad training decreases those odds. We have a maxim that we lean on,

Good training is better than no training, no training is better than bad training.

Good training essentially compounds our abilities and our confidence levels. Bad training might negatively influence our abilities whilst still compounding our confidence levels, this will allow us to take risks that we are not necessarily prepared for. No training leaves it up to chance. It doesn't mean the resolution will favor us - simply that we aren't decreasing whichever odds we were dealt at the start of the incident.

Getting back to our mock incident in the bar. The training, whether good, bad or nonexistent, will very tangibly influence both men's' abilities and their confidence levels. This will in turn influence their willingness and reluctance to fight as well as their actual ability to do so effectively. Once again, if you don't know the guy in front of you, you have no idea what training he brings to the game. You might think you are up against a regular Joe, only to find out the guy is hard as nails and knows exactly what he is doing.

Interestingly, this dynamic also comes into play with violent crime. Although your average criminal's ability and opportunities to train differs from a regular Joe, you will be surprised to find that they still do train. Many criminal subcultures have training and development methods and processes entrenched into their societal structures. The training may look different, and not be as effective or as elegant as what is available to a regular Joe, but it might still be there.

Remember, with violent crime, criminals are career orientated. They want to succeed, obviously for profit, but also because if they don't, they either get injured, killed or incarcerated. As such, they develop methods for counteracting these risks.

MOTIVATION

Motivation is one of the more difficult concepts for those new to the study of violence to understand. Motivation levels differ and fluctuate. How committed one person is to making AND successfully completing an attack differs from the next. Consider this anecdote from Schalk:

I remember as a young man getting into my first fist fight after moving to a big city. A couple of minutes (yes, it was a long fight) into the incident my opponent pulls away from me, looks me in the eye, and says "you're hitting me but I'm not feeling anything." Now at that stage I was too young and uninitiated to call him out on it. Rather I let it get to me and I immediately lost my motivation. Another way of putting this is that my brain switched from a limbic fight response to a limbic flight response. What was a good brawl turned into a defensive fight for me and I got my ass kicked.

Certain aggressors will go all the way, others will back off in the face of a show or threat of force, others will feint and come back with a vengeance, frequently on their terms and by multiplying their own ability to apply force (think weapons and friends). Even during the CCI one guy might take a punch or two and then throw in the towel, another might stay in it regardless of how hard a beating he is getting, conversely another might continue beating or stabbing you long after the necessity for it has passed.

Motivation both differs and fluctuates for every person at any given time.

OTHER FACTORS

Other important factors, and there are definitely more, that increase this complexity in no particular order are:

• Frame or state of mind

• Agenda

• Substance use or abuse

• Psychological problems

• Pain tolerance

• Fear

The aim of this section is to help you understand that the incident itself has many contributing factors. Factors that are already there and present as the incident is developing. It is a challenge for someone that has not been the target and/or victim of such an incident to fully grasp our need to respect this complexity. The reality is that we just don't ever really know exactly who this person in front of us is, or what they are capable of. For some of us we don't even fully know ourselves or what we are capable of yet either.

And we need to nurture a healthy respect for this.

VIOLENCE IS EXTREMELY DYNAMIC

In this context we are using the term extremely dynamic to denote the idea that things change very fast and continuously in a violent incident. There is no real script as to exactly how the incident will develop. We can attempt to project our script onto the incident but we have no guarantee that the script is accurate to start with, or that the incident will stick to the script as it progresses. The incident has no care or feelings for or about your script.

Let's look at certain primary factors that lead to this extreme dynamism.

ENVIRONMENTAL CHANGES

Environmental changes pertain specifically to the space in which the incident is taking place. This would include the space dimensions, basic layout, as well any and all objects within the space.

In terms of the type of space: The room, or environment, may change as an incident travels from one room to another, or from inside a building to the outside. Different rooms or environments will contain different objects. Objects that were not present in the previous environment and as such, objects which your brain hasn't mapped out yet. Furniture, equipment, gardens, curbs, vehicles; all of these can change as the environment changes.

The actual size of the space might also change. You might have a large open space in which to function only to be forced into a small and tight space. As we'll more fully develop later: Weapons, and as such Techniques, have active ranges in which they are functional. Change the size of the space and you possibly change effective Techniques and Tactics.

SITUATIONAL CHANGES

These changes pertain to anything which fundamentally changes the type of situation that we are dealing with.

Thinking about our standoff in the bar from earlier. Person A might be very alert, focused and ready for whatever next step he has planned. He might have been perfectly prepared to surprise Person B with a right cross to the jaw. Right at the last moment, and too late in this incident, he picks up on a flash of movement to his left. Before his brain even orients itself accurately he's struck in the neck by Person B's best friend who was sneaking up on him from the side. Person A most definitely could have and should have accounted for the possibility of a second opponent. It's his own fault he did not, so no excuses for him. The situation changed and he missed it. But this is a very basic and accessible example of a situational change to the incident. Alternatively, Person A might have projected a peaceful resolution to the incident. In his mind he might have been making progress. Person B seems to have become a bit more quiet and withdrawn. Mistaking an adrenalin dump for submission he is caught completely by surprise when Person B suddenly and aggressively assaults him. This touches on the next topic of internal changes, Person B underwent an internal change, whilst Person A missed it and now had to respond to the situational change.

Lastly, the actual positions of the participants may change as well. Regardless of whether they started the incident standing, sitting, kneeling or lying down, this starting position or levels may easily change.

INTERNAL CHANGES

Let us start with a disclaimer. Neither myself, nor any of the contributors to this study, are medical practitioners or professional academic researchers.

That said, internal changes pertain to the effects of certain inter-related chemical (hormonal), biometric and neurological changes which occur under certain conditions. In one sense most of this book is dedicated to one key internal change: how brain functioning changes in the CCI. The bulk of this book's content is focused on these changes as they strongly influence our approach to developing combative Tactics and solutions.

In terms of the category of biometrical changes, so much research has been done that we don't feel pressed to offer a comprehensive treatment on the topic. We offer this schematic as summary of one of these research pieces:

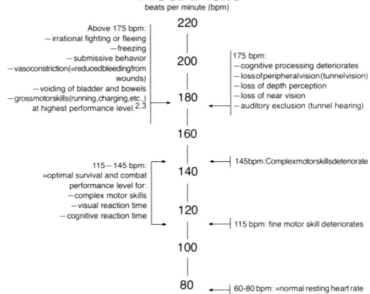

Reprinted from The Post-Traumatic Gazette © Patience H. C. Mason   Volume 4 , Number 4, Nov/Dec 1998

Effects of Hormonal Induced Heart Rate Increase [1]

©1997 Siddle & Grosssssman
reprinted with permission

HeartRate
beats per minute (bpm)

220

175 bpm:
—cognitive processing deteriorates
—loss of peripheral vision (tunnel vision)
—loss of depth perception
—loss of near vision
— auditory exclusion (tunnel hearing)

200

Above 175 bpm:
— irrational fighting or fleeing
—freezing
— submissive behavior
—vasoconstriction(=reducedbleedingfrom wounds)
—voiding of bladder and bowels
—grossmotorskills(running,charging,etc.) at highest performance level.[2,3]

180

160

140   145bpm: Complex motor skills deteriorate

115—145 bpm:
=optimal survival and combat performance level for:
—complex motor skills
—visual reaction time
—cognitive reaction time

120

115 bpm: fine motor skill deteriorates

100

80   60-80 bpm: =normal resting heart rate

Notes
1—This data is for hormonal induced heart rate increases resulting from sympathetic nervous system arousal. Exercise induced increases will not have the same effect.
2—Hormonal induced performance and strength increases can achieve 100% of potential max within 10 seconds, but drop to 55% after 30 seconds, 35% after 60 seconds and 31% after 90 seconds. It takes a minimum of 3 minutes rest to "recharge" the system.
3—Any extended period of relaxation after intense sympathetic nervous system arousal can result in a parasympathetic backlash, with significant drops in energy level, heart rate and blood pressure. This can manifest itself as normal shock symptoms (dizziness, nausea and/or vomiting, paleness, clammy skin) and/or profound exhaustion.

From an academic point of view, we would be very interested to do or see any well documented research on the correlations between these heart rate changes and the changes in brain function. As Rory Miller rightly says:

You are fighting a mind, not just a body." As such it makes sense that we understand what happens to that mind under these conditions. [Miller, Rory. Facing Violence: Preparing for the Unexpected (Kindle Locations 3025-3029). YMAA Publication Center. Kindle Edition.]

VIOLENCE HAS AN UNPREDICTABLE OUTCOME

Let's recap our definition of the Nature of Violence:

Violence is inherently complex, extremely dynamic, and as such, has an unpredictable outcome.

It is the previous two components of the Nature of Violence that leads us here. It is BECAUSE violence is inherently complex AND extremely dynamic that we say it has an unpredictable outcome. We can never really guarantee whether a violent incident will end in the way we expected it to. Let me (Schalk) relate some anecdotes to drive the point home:

When I was a teenager, a friend and myself accosted another teen that was showing too much interest in a certain girl at school. My friend head-butted the other guy once on the nose. The other guy keeled over backwards and started convulsing – blood, foam and vomitus coming out of his mouth and nose. I proceeded to pick up my own and my friend's suitcase and we flat out made a run for it. (The other guy made it through fine.) We obviously didn't think it was going to end like that.

One evening, I got into an argument with a guy at a club. It was over complete nonsense and I was way out of line. At one stage he said he was going to shoot me if I carry on. The moment he said it I knocked him out. I left him on the floor there and continued with my evening. Later that evening, when I left the club, he came running at me with his pistol pointed at me. I luckily dodged a couple of bullets that night by circling around a vehicle, back into the club, out the back and over the fence of the clubs' rear yard.

One day, I was intervening in an attempted kidnapping. The perpetrator was busy forcing a victim into a vehicle whilst she was screaming and fighting to get out, fearfully crying for help. On approaching he immediately decided to come at me. I was unarmed but lethal use of force was not apt as yet in any case. As he came for me I struck him with a perfectly aimed elbow. It would have knocked him out if he didn't raise his hand to grab at me right at the last moment. I was quite a lot taller than him and as such his hand needed to raise above his neckline where the elbow was aimed at. As such, this newly raised hand blocked the incoming elbow and much of that elbow's initial force was dissipated into the blocking hand. I had no way of knowing that would happen. An incident that could have resolved in that moment turned into full blown CCI. We had a positive resolution but the CCI went on much longer than I anticipated or desired.

All of us have anecdotes. Some more and less violent and intense than any or all of these. We respect that and we definitely are not sharing these without purpose. We are sharing these anecdotes purely to help readers who haven't been exposed to violence to understand its nature.

Kindly remember that, as we said before, these lists are by no means meant to be exhaustive. We have added the main categories of influencers and populated them to some extent, the purpose of the chapter is to impress upon the uninitiated reader the reality of the Nature of Violence; when it comes to violence and especially in a CCI, we honestly have no idea of predicting exactly what the outcome will be.

CHAPTER 3: DUELS, ASSAULTS & ENDEMICS

One critical part of understanding the Close Combat Incident (CCI) relates to what it looks like and what it does not. The problem though is that the image we have in our minds can be influenced by a variety of sources. Sources which aren't necessarily guaranteed to give us a correct or sensible viewpoint. Movies and popular culture, our instructors, other students in the class, social media, etc. can all be influencing factors in what we think the CCI will look like. This can create huge risk for us if our idea of the CCI differs much from reality.

The old saying "train how you fight" has almost become a mantra for many training enthusiasts. Risking being accused of semantical tricks, we would actually like to adapt that to "train for what you will have to fight." To do so however we first need to bring to light some of the potential issues that might be dragging us off point.

Apart from the very last chapter in the book, this is probably the other chapter in which we can offend the most readers at once. Kindly understand that it is not our intention to step on anyone's toes. Everyone is permitted to have their own opinion, everyone isn't permitted to have their own facts. As with everything else in this book, we are committed to deal in facts, not opinions or anecdotes.

DUELS VS. ASSAULTS

What is an assault? Rory Miller offers us the following apt description:

Someone is trying to kill you. Even if the intent is not lethal, the Threat is trying to deliver as much force as he can to your body. He is not feeding you a technique. He is also not setting up a layered combination in order to create an opening. The Threat is beating you down. Unlike sparring he will not be holding back either to protect you from injury or his fists from injury or to keep his defense up. His defense is that he is doing so much damage to you so fast that you can't think beyond that. This is how an assault works. [Miller, Rory. Facing Violence: Preparing for the Unexpected (Kindle Locations 2935-2941). YMAA Publication Centre. Kindle Edition.]

It is our contention that the main elephant in the martial art and combative training environment's living room is the fact that individuals are NOT training for assaults. We specifically frame this statement as NOT training for assaults instead of training for duels, as there is actually one more issue that is cropping up more and more, and that is training against stationary Opponents. Neither of these two options resemble the dynamics of an assault.

Depending on the Trainee's context (and bearing in mind this book doesn't cover sport fighting) he will probably face one of three types of Opponent: A submissive Opponent (in which case we probably wouldn't be applying much force), an Opponent resistant (and possibly combative) to control or arrest, or an Opponent that assaults them. The resistant Opponent might attempt to duel the Trainee, but the Trainee should in no way be dueling back. If the Opponent is assaulting the Trainee then Trainee cannot duel as dueling tactics aren't effective against assaults.

None of this means that a duel is less dangerous or less violent than an assault. It is simply a different problem contextually. Duels are a dispute solving mechanism wherein the participants will solve their differences of opinion in a trial by combat. Assaults are purely damage causing mechanisms. There are places in the world where this type of dispute solving mechanism is culturally very rooted. Historically, in certain societies, there were duels by firearm or edged weapons. We still find these duels in present day, but most societies have downgraded to some form of hand to hand combat.

Why does knowing the difference matter? Because many people are stuck in a dueling mentality without realizing it. The problem is that some dueling arts and skills don't have immediate or fast incident resolution as its primary outcome. Remember that dueling is actually a form of social violence. It might be that the outcome of the duel is to kill the other person, but frequently it's not. Frequently the outcome of the duel is only to submit, embarrass or maim the other party.

Currently, many weapon based martial arts and combative systems are actually dueling arts. This doesn't mean the Techniques are necessarily bad or shouldn't be used, but the dueling context has influenced the Tactics and application of the Techniques. Again, you cannot effectively respond to an assault with a dueling mindset. If your martial arts or combative training stems from a cultural background where dueling is/was commonplace then, there's a good chance you are dueling as well. Simply consider the Tactics and adjust where you need to.

At the risk of stepping on toes, but as a practical example, let's consider the Filipino Martial Arts. Many of its Techniques and Tactics lean towards dueling.

This doesn't mean they can't be applied elsewhere. It's simply the FMA cultural context. FMA originates from a society where it was commonplace to use dueling to settle disputes, especially dueling with certain types of weapons. That said, these duels were not always intended to be lethal, but more to establish dominance or to educate. Once you understand this, a lot of the FMA Techniques and Tactics make a lot of sense. Does this mean FMA is bad? Or flawed? Or unusable? No, not at all. Just understand the context and the effect it might have on your preparation for CCIs.

Fundamentally, regardless of whether we are talking about FMA or even about fist fighting, the issue is this: Transplanting a system that is designed to deal with a dispute and using it to deal with an assault is going to create some critical breakdowns when trying to resolve the CCI.

Our recommendation is that you research the origin of your training, as well as comparing whether your training environment is based on the three types of Opponents listed above. Afterwards consider your training methodology and ask yourself if the Techniques, and more specifically the Tactics in their application would be useful against a committed assault.

ENDEMICS

Endemic is defined as a characteristic of (or prevalent in) a particular field, area, or environment. In the context of this book it refers to the Tactics as well as the combative methods and styles used by criminals or other parties from a specific location.

The word endemics has been trending in the combatives community during the last couple of years, and especially so in social media circles. What we are seeing more and more, is that people are adopting endemics without understanding context. It has almost become cool to do so. Unfortunately there is a rapidly growing community of close combat practitioners that are glorifying criminal tactics and lifestyles without having any depth of understanding as to whether, where and when, those tactics are sensible or not.

Simply banking on street credibility to prove an approach is sensible is idiotic. Place one firearm wielding gangster in a building with a well trained SWAT operative and take a guess who's walking out.

Furthermore, criminal Tactics have very specific outcomes and the application of their Techniques have been shaped by these outcomes.

Take the Piper system as an example.

Piper's claim to fame is the systematizing of the knife culture used in the Cape Flats in South Africa. It is purported as stemming first hand from interaction with South African gangsters. For reasons beyond the scope of this book, these claims, as well as the corresponding international trend of glorifying criminal and gang cultures, are generating a large following in the online community. The Piper system however is first and foremost a deception-based assassination system. Is it effective in what it aims to achieve? Yes, most definitely. But it begs the question: What context would the Trainee find themselves in, in which they need to actively maintain medium to close range with an Opponent, and then deceive the Opponent long enough, and in such a way, as to effectively assassinate them? If that is truly your context then Piper is a very good option. If it is not your context, congratulations, you are going to jail. Furthermore, the Piper system is perfect for pro-active use of the knife. But it is very underdeveloped for tactical or defensive application. By defensive we mean that an assault is in process and you have to actively manage the incoming energy and force.

When we start evaluating in this way, honestly and soberly, we can see that certain trending systems contain flaws when using tactically, defensively and/or legally. That isn't to say they don't contain Tactics that are useful, or that they don't have Techniques which aren't useful to know. It's just important to think and use our minds to evaluate where and why specific systems or approaches are useful and where and why not. Be careful of simply adopting what's currently trending on social media. Being a very practical person, take this example from Gavin, one of the authors of this book:

I have lived all my life in Cape Town, no more than 10-15 minute drive from the Cape Flats. The Cape Flats include some of the most violent neighborhoods in the city. Many of the people I went to high school with were gang members and came from the Flats. However, my experience of the Cape Flats gang style knife assassinations is nonexistent, because it's a problem that typically doesn't leave its cultural home. If my life had taken a different turn and had I become involved in gangsterism, then it may have been more like something I should worry about, because contextually it lives in that specific endemic environment. It's a style associated with solving a very specific problem, in a very specific place. Taking it out of its context and applying it to your civilian self defense situation is like learning to scuba dive to better prepare you for a high altitude mountain expedition - just because both activities have oxygen tanks involved doesn't make it the same thing.

We reiterate. It's not that we cannot learn from or shouldn't take time to understand endemics, but actual dynamic CCIs are what we are training for, and those are controlled by the brain and understanding the brain has universal instead of only geographic relevance. Any Techniques or Tactics that we train in should be selected and developed specifically for these CCIs, and we should apply this type of thinking to whichever martial art or combative system we are considering. Understand that system's context, where it came from, where it lives in and what would be the benefits or consequences of transplanting into your own context. Understand its cultural background and what problems it was intended to solve, and then ask yourself if it will work to solve the problems in your own reality.

PART TWO – DEFINING THE PROBLEM

CHAPTER FOUR: THE TWO SYSTEMS

THE TRIUNE BRAIN MODEL

For decades the three brain system has dominated the world of combatives and self defense. The proposition that we have three separate parts of the brain, each controlling three distinctly different sets of functions and types of reactions, was rooted in Paul D. Maclean's Triune Brain model originally formulated in the 1960's.

Very simply, Maclean suggested three complexes in the brain, he termed these the Reptilian Complex, the Paleomammalian Complex and the Neomammalian Complex respectively. This was subsequently simplified into the Reptile Brain, the Monkey Brain and the Human Brain. Each of the complexes does and would, under certain conditions, guide, control, and/or attempt to control aspects of our physiology and/or behavior. The Triune Brain model provided an easily accessible way of understanding why individuals experienced certain behaviors under certain conditions.

It is important to understand that when Maclean suggested his hypothesis that we did not have the luxury of MRIs available, i.e. it was not possible to monitor the brain's activity and to establish the correctness of his claims. Maclean's work was influenced by other academics from the 20th century and was made popular through one of Carl Sagan's books (1977 Pulitzer Prize winning *The Dragons of Eden*) as well as Maclean's own *The Triune Brain in Evolution* published in 1990.

We have since seen many technological advancements allowing us to monitor the brain under natural and simulated conditions. From this capability the following two similar but distinct points have emerged. Both are key to understand and assimilate into our thinking:

• **There are no three brains**. Although this could technically be seen in anatomical studies (three structures were observed, not three brains) it is now confirmed through observing the brain's functioning through MRIs.

• **There are no three completely distinct areas in which thinking takes place**. Meaning, that there are no circumstances within which the brain operates COMPLETELY SEPARATELY within Maclean's three suggested complexes.

So what are we learning?

• **The brain is significantly more integrated than what was previously thought**. Even though certain types of thinking, sensing, experiencing, responding etc. does show more actively in different parts of the brain it is by no means completely separated from the rest of the brain.

• **However, the brain does display two distinct types of functioning**. Even though these two types of functioning, which we will be referring to as two different systems, are quite distinct, they should also not be thought of as two uniquely separate entities, as if there are two individuals calling the shots in your brain, i.e. we should not replace the Triune Brain Model with a new dual brain model.

The reality of what we are learning from the most recent neuroscience requires us to ask certain questions:

1. What should we be learning from these newest developments for the combative and self defense environments?

2. Can these developments positively impact our training methods? And if so,

3. How should these developments influence our training methods?

This book is a systematic, research and experienced based attempt, to answer these three questions. As technology advances we are able to more clearly see and start to understand what is happening to the brain under specific conditions. We are able to dissect this knowledge, learn from it, and formulate better solutions for the combative and self defense environments. In one of the author's previously owned companies, we spent 18 months to redevelop our training methodologies to better fit these two systems. This book is very much based on what we have found leading up to and during that time.

But, it requires us to shift our thinking away from the Triune Brain model to the Two Systems model. We will however, for the purpose of this book and ease of communication, refer to the limbic system every now and again. The limbic system contribution to the academic society interestingly enough also belongs to Maclean. Some see it as his most noteworthy contribution to society. We note this now so that its use later in the book doesn't appear contradictory to our abandonment of the Triune Brain Model.

We would like to cite Rory Miller in relation to the Triune Brain model. Before we do so, kindly note that we have nothing but respect for Rory Miller. We have read much of his work and he has always been a positive influence in our own growth and development; we are truly grateful to Rory for the impact he has made in our and many others' lives. That said though, we have to now reconsider statements like these:

I used the monkey analogy many, many times. Once you learn to see it, little primate power plays are everywhere. For the most part they are petty, nasty, and unpleasant, but the operant word is "petty." You don't need to play. If there is one thing that can lead humans to a higher, more effective and conscious way of dealing with the universe it will be learning to see when they are acting like monkeys and to choose when it is and isn't appropriate. Both monkeys need to play for the game to work. [Miller, Rory. Facing Violence: Preparing for the Unexpected (Kindle Locations 4086-4099). YMAA Publication Center. Kindle Edition.]

The challenge in citing this paragraph, is that if we were to be honest about it, we have used this model as a teaching aid ourselves for many, many years. Citing this paragraph also runs the risk of not giving a holistic picture of everything Rory Miller and his associates teach around the topic. Meaning, we know that they actually develop this theme more fully, including presenting and integrating more recent research, when they provide training.

However, returning to the treatment of this chapter, the first thing we need to do is to reconsider the Triune Brain "category" of the monkey itself. Does it exist? From a neuroscience point of view - no it doesn't. Do we see the behavior that Rory Miller is describing? Most definitely. Thus the issue is not with the observations but with the model through which they have been interpreted. We are in no sense trying to refute Rory Miller - his observations are spot on. The fact that observations get re-evaluated through new research is actually okay and happens quite frequently in the scientific community. For this reason, it is our observation and contention that the behaviors placed within the "monkey" and "reptile" categories both relate to a specific system of functioning that we will be discussing throughout this book, and that we should start attributing it as such.

Some of you might ask whether we cannot just keep these terms? To be honest, in our training experience, the Triune Brain model makes a sensible teaching aid. People seem to intrinsically "get" or "associate" what you are trying to communicate with the Triune Brain terminology. Is it wise though? No. We honestly don't think so.

The Triune Brain model was proposed in an era before we understood concepts like neuroplasticity - the brain's ability to physically change structure in response to stimulus. With the Triune Brain model we were stuck - our brains were subconsciously seen to be unchangeable. We had to understand the three

Brains and learn to work with them. They were in control. However, understanding neuroplasticity, as well as the Two Systems model we'll be introducing you to, we now realise we are able to actually program our brains for much better decision making and performance under pressure.

What was once understood to be unchangeable Monkey and Reptile brain reactions, we are now finding to be programmable System 1 and System 2 reactions. Thus, apart from the simple fact that we are faced with new research findings, and as such we need to contend with it honestly and with integrity, we have seen the worth in adopting these findings and adapting our training to it. And as we progress through this book you will hopefully start to notice why we are saying so.

But let us first introduce you to the Two Systems in a very concise and hopefully accessible manner.

INTRODUCTION TO THE TWO SYSTEMS

Many researchers are now advocating for a dual-system mode of thinking. The automatic system is fast, automatic, effortless, and emotional, and uses tacit knowledge. The reflective system is slower, conscious, effortful, deliberate, logical, and serial, and uses explicit knowledge. These two systems, which work in different ways, complement each other, just as the rod cells and cone cells in our eyes complement each other. The two systems are different mental gears that we can use. [Klein, Gary. Streetlights and Shadows: Searching for the Keys to Adaptive Decision Making (MIT Press) (p. 93). The MIT Press. Kindle Edition.]

Before I start, Gary Klein, the author of many books including *Streetlights and Shadows: Searching for the Keys to Adaptive Decision Making*, from which the above has been cited, is probably one of the more accessible researchers and authors you should be reading if you want to take your knowledge on the topic deeper. Contrasting with him we have Daniel Kahneman, from which we will also be citing regularly in this book, that you need to look into. Although Daniel Kahneman's work is also accessible, his books are much denser, technical, and he shares a phenomenal amount of research and findings through them. The specific book that you can start with that relates to this study is titled *Thinking, Fast and Slow*. Both authors are well informed, leading from the front in my opinion, as well as being great communicators. You should definitely look into both, however, if time is an issue or you just want a more concise and accessible romp, go for Klein. If you have time and you are a detail orientated person go for Kahneman. Be aware though that violence is not their primary study field so you will need to use your own mind to interpret it accordingly.

Thanks to Kahneman, these two systems popularly became known as and referred to simply as System 1 and System 2. We will adopt and use these terms. System 1 is summarized by Klein as operating "automatically and quickly, with little or no effort and no sense of voluntary control," and System 2 as the function which "allocates attention to the effortful mental activities that demand it, including complex computations. The operations of System 2 are often associated with the subjective experience of agency, choice and concentration."

It was whilst reading Daniel Kahneman that I first discovered the distinction that with System 1 "thinking is happening," and with System 2 "I am thinking." This by no means implies that Kahneman or ourselves are suggesting that System 1 is in some way not me. Purely that with System 1 thinking is directed from a more non conscious faculty; System 2 is wholly conscious and when it is active it is because I am actively thinking.

Kahneman gives us ways to think about the two Systems in the following list:

In rough order of complexity, here are some examples of the automatic activities that are attributed to System 1:

- *Detect that one object is more distant than another.*
- *Orient to the source of a sudden sound.*
- *Complete the phrase "bread and …"*
- *Make a "disgust face" when shown a horrible picture. • Detect hostility in a voice.*
- *Answer to 2 + 2 = ?*
- *Read words on large billboards.*
- *Drive a car on an empty road.*
- *Find a strong move in chess (if you are a chess master).*
- *Understand simple sentences.*
- *Recognise that a "meek and tidy soul with a passion for detail" resembles an occupational stereotype.*

The highly diverse operations of System 2 have one feature in common: they require attention and are disrupted when attention is drawn away. Here are some examples:

- *Brace for the starter gun in a race.*
- *Focus attention on the clowns in the circus.*
- *Focus on the voice of a particular person in a crowded and noisy room.*

- *Look for a woman with white hair.*
- *Search memory to identify a surprising sound.*
- *Maintain a faster walking speed than is natural for you.*
- *Count the occurrences of the letter a in a page of text.*
- *Monitor the appropriateness of your behavior in a social situation.*
- *Tell someone your phone number.*
- *Park in a narrow space (for most people except garage attendants).*
- *Compare two washing machines for overall value.*
- *Fill out a tax form.*
- *Check the validity of a complex logical argument.*

In all these situations you must pay attention, and you will perform less well, or not at all, if you are not ready or if your attention is directed inappropriately. System 2 has some ability to change the way System 1 works, by programming the normally automatic functions of attention and memory.[Kahneman, Daniel. Thinking, Fast and Slow (p. 21-22). Penguin Books Ltd. Kindle Edition.]

Our most basic question then obviously is what does all of this mean for the study of combatives and self defense? The following questions are apparent:

- Do these systems run at the same time? Or do they switch back and forth? How would the answer to this question influence needed reactions and responses to a critical incident?
- Where do our combative reactions, skills or responses reside - System 1 or System 2?
- Does acting pro-actively in a combative or self defense situation lie in a different system than re-acting to incoming stimulus, i.e. does searching, deciding and responding lie in a different system than reacting?
- Are there tactics and other procedures, techniques and skills, that function completely or better in one or the other System?
- And most importantly, if so, can we train them specifically in and for that system? And what training methodologies would give us the best success?

As we progress we will be grappling with these questions. However, it is our contention that for all types of Close Combat Incidents (CCIs), the critical issue lies with our ability to fight effectively in System 1. The second but no less important critical issue lies with our ability to train and optimize System 1 for CCIs. Why is this our contention? In a nutshell it relates to Kahneman's essential position: System 1 is fast. System 2 is slow.

THE IMPORTANCE OF SYSTEM 1

Note that the rapid decision making and reaction relating to an ambush are System 1 functions. This means, under ambush conditions System 1 will be in charge of the immediate and first response. Furthermore during the CCI, and whilst being exposed to the extreme dynamism of violence, it's important to understand that there is a very high speed and volume of incoming information to which your brain will consistently need to adapt, under these constantly changing conditions System 1 will also continue to remain in charge.

On that initial ambush encounter see what Kahneman says:

System 1 has been shaped by evolution to provide a continuous assessment of the main problems that an organism must solve to survive: How are things going? Is there a threat or a major opportunity? Is everything normal? Should I approach or avoid? The questions are perhaps less urgent for a human in a city environment than for a gazelle on the savannah, but we have inherited the neural mechanisms that evolved to provide ongoing assessments of threat level, and they have not been turned off. Situations are constantly evaluated as good or bad, requiring escape or permitting approach. [Kahneman, Daniel. Thinking, Fast and Slow (p. 90). Penguin Books Ltd. Kindle Edition.]

The same immediate and extremely fast mental process driving the reaction of a gazelle to an ambush by a lion, is the same mental process that we'll experience when ambushed by a criminal in a dark alley. Later, when we touch on issues like time-frames in CCIs you are going to notice how short these encounters truly are, and as such, how fast you need to be able to perform. System 1 is highly adapted to work at these incredible speeds. Klein also gives us insight into System 1's incredible abilities when he refers to it as intuition: The ability to make certain judgment calls rapidly and without consciously thinking about it. Note that even though Klein doesn't specifically use the terminology of System 1, he is clearly talking about the brain's mode of functioning where "thinking is happening":

Intuition isn't a magical property. I am defining intuition as ways we use our experience without consciously thinking things out. Intuition includes tacit knowledge that we can't describe. It includes our ability to recognize patterns stored in memory. We have been building these patterns up for decades, and we can rapidly match a situation to a pattern or notice that something is off— that some sort of anomaly is warning us to be careful.[Klein, Gary. Streetlights and Shadows: Searching for the Keys to Adaptive Decision Making (MIT Press) (p.

71). The MIT Press. Kindle Edition.]

To summarize then: System 1 is highly adapted to work at the speeds we'll be re-acting and responding at under CCI conditions. As we will find though, it doesn't mean that simply because System 1 is fast that it is effective. The reality that we have to contend with is the following: Whether we are trained to operate well in System 1 or not, under certain conditions, our brains will switch to System 1. This will Switch will occur whether we like it or not. This should impress upon us that not only do we WANT to be able to perform well in System 1, we actually HAVE to be able to perform well in System 1. For these reasons, it will be highly beneficial for us to train System 1 to operate at its most effective during a CCI.

The next chapter will introduce you to what we'll call the Switch.

THE MAUL

CHAPTER FIVE: THE SWITCH

We use the term the Switch, or Switching, interchangeably. Its importance to us relates both to the thresholds and the timing under which the brain switches to and fro between System 1 and System 2. Reminding ourselves about the fact that the brain's functioning is generally very integrated, on a technical level then, there isn't actually a clearly delineated switch happening. What we mean by this is that there is no imaginary toggle switch with a System 1 Mode left and System 2 Mode right as if these modes of functioning are completely separated from each other. That said however, there are very clear conditions under which the brain prefers to function from System 1 rather than System 2 or vice versa - and the moment that the brain moves over to one or the other's mode of functioning is the moment we call the Switch. However, for the purpose of this book, we'll be referring to the Switch as if it was a very clearly delineated event. As you'll see below, we are able to gain insight into these conditions using a couple of different frameworks or approaches. For our application we will mostly be considering when the brain switches from System 2 to System 1. Note again what Kahneman teaches (emphasis added):

Orienting and responding quickly to the gravest threats or most promising opportunities improved the chance of survival, and this capability is certainly not restricted to humans. Even in modern humans, System 1 takes over in emergencies and assigns total priority to self-protective actions. Imagine yourself at the wheel of a car that unexpectedly skids on a large oil slick. You will find that you have responded to the threat before you became fully conscious of it. [Kahneman, Daniel. Thinking, Fast and Slow (p. 35). Penguin Books Ltd. Kindle Edition.]

Let us introduce you to another concept before progressing, it is called the Threshold. We use this term to indicate the imaginary line in the sand, the trigger break moment, when the Switch occurs. Technically, it's a set of correct conditions, which having been met, forces the Switch to occur. Hence, if we "step" over the Threshold the Switch occurs. Although the factors involved in the Switch are the same for every human, the Threshold for every individual is unique. That is, if the factor relates to volume for example, each and every person's capacity for volume is different. Thresholds, luckily, can be influenced and enhanced through accurate training. Because of this, we can move the Threshold into a direction beneficial to us, but we can never truly escape the Switch. Nor should we aim to, there are conditions under which System 1 is going to be the most helpful. The Switch is fundamentally part of our physiology in the same sense as, for example, an increase in respiratory rate will affect an increase in heart rate. We should simply understand it and aim to use it to our benefit.

ON FACTORS AND THRESHOLDS

FACTOR 1: SPEED OF INCOMING DATA (SPEED)

This issue relates specifically to how fast events are happening or progressing around you. It's the essential problem with an ambush, or a deceptive assassination attempt, the attack is structured to circumvent your ability to re-act or respond accurately by its rapidity. It's also the essential problem with, say for instance, a committed relentless assault (regardless of weapon used). In both cases, continuous or progressing events are moving too fast for System 2 so System 1 attempts to manage them. Placing the distinction between the two dynamics within a practical context: An ambush might be a single stab with a knife. A committed relentless assault might be multiple stabs with a knife. Whether there are single or multiple stabs, both are happening too fast for System 2 to deal with.

FACTOR 2: VOLUME OF INCOMING DATA (VOLUME)

Very closely related to the issue of speed is the issue of volume. Now there are too many things happening at once or in fast succession. Because the volume is higher, it essentially also becomes a problem of speed as the brain is still simply struggling to keep up. An apt example here might be two attackers or opponents attacking simultaneously. Another example might be an assault where the direction of the incoming attack is constantly changing leaving the brain no chance to adapt to a pattern. Even if their attack was launched a tad slower than a solo attacker, the brain, for example, has twice the amount of data to process and as such only half the time in which to do so.

FACTOR 3: DANGER VS. FEAR (DANGER, FEAR)

As we've clearly noticed up until now, System 1 is strongly tasked with our survival. For this reason, the Switch will also initiate when sensing danger, frequently before System 2 has noticed that it has lost control. A flinch response to an attack is a very good example of a Switch where System 1 takes over. A flinch response is a very high speed reaction to an act or event the brain has identified as being dangerous. Please note, not necessarily a hostile event, just a perceived dangerous event, e.g. a friend throws a ball at your head whilst you were looking away, your eye catches it at last moment, and you flinch. System 1 is also highly aroused by fear. Fear, traditionally, should be closely connected to actual danger. Unfortunately we live in a society where few people experience true danger. This, along with other complex societal dynamics outside of the scope of this book's treatment, has created a disconnect between danger and fear. This disconnect can cause unnecessary Switches in individuals with various fear related issues.

FACTOR 4: HEIGHTENED EMOTIONAL STATE (EMOTIONS)

In line with our brief touch on fear, other emotional states can also push one closer to the Threshold. Think about a person experiencing anger, losing control of their fully conscious faculties, and going Switching over to a very reactive mode of functioning. This reactive mode of functioning may be verbally abusive, physically aggressive, or any number of other reactions, whichever it may be, in a certain sense they have "lost control". Or consider someone experiencing fear when confronted with certain stimulus, and suddenly having to contend with unwarranted thoughts and interpretations on the event, possibly even a sudden flight response causing them to run away. A heightened emotional state pushes one closer to the Threshold. It is important to note though that the actual heightened emotional state is NOT a Switch, it does not mean a Switch has or even needs to occur. This is a very important distinction to make and keep in mind as the more we mature in this aspect the longer we can stay in System 2. We will touch on why this can be beneficial later in the chapter.

ON THE TIMING OF THE SWITCH

In a very simplified analogy, we can refer to System 1 as an autopilot. It is preprogrammed. It runs off scripts or algorithms of which some are hardwired and others programmable. When the Switch occurs, whatever has been coded into System 1 will take over. If System 1 offers no sensible option it will quite possibly revert to a Limbic Response (freeze, flight or fight). We won't delve too much into the Limbic Responses as others have already done a lot of great work on the topic. For the scope of this book, and at the risk of mixing non related research and writings, it's just important to understand the following very rough and loose order:

We would prefer the brain in System 2 until we are happy to Switch, however, if a threshold is crossed it will Switch to System 1 whether we like or not, and lastly, when System 1 is not providing a sensible solution it will revert to a Limbic Response.

All of this happens at extremely high speeds and for the uneducated the Switch might even be missed. However, we have developed specific drills that clearly and repeatedly display the order mentioned above.

The primary factors listed above relate to both the understanding and the training to extend the Threshold of the Switch, and in doing so, to remain in System 2 for as long as possible. Even though we said this chapter is focused on the Switch from System 2 to System 1, this does not mean we necessarily want to switch. There are certain abilities in System 2 which are very useful in CCIs.

BENEFITS OF SYSTEM 2

1. **Better logical decision making in the absence of inadequate training and experience**. Very simply, if System 1 has not been trained and equipped to deal with a specific type of situation, then there is arguably more value in maintaining System 2's logical faculties.

2. **Better emotional and impulse control**. Another way to think about System 1 and System 2 is to borrow and transplant the analogy of a bull and a bull rider into this topic. This analogy first came to our attention from another author and within the context of aggression and self control, however, we unfortunately cannot remember who and from where. Imagine System 1 is a bucking bull still contained behind the bucking chute's gate, mounted and ready to be ridden. System 2 is the cowboy mounted and waiting for the gate to open. Whilst the gate is closed System 2 is completely in control. Opening the gate and releasing the bull can be likened to an immense dump of emotional energy - fear or rage for example. However, the rider can still ride the bull, or rather, System 2 can still remain in control of System 1. Should the rider lose control though it would be as if System 1 has now completely taken over. System 1 is able to provide and function efficiently alongside a tremendous amount of emotional or

chemical energy - energy which might fuel the aggression needed to fight or the stamina needed to run away. But that emotional energy unleashed too fast, in the wrong way, or untrained, might actually escalate whatever situation you are trying to successfully negotiate, and possibly even destroy the bull rider.

3. **Better accuracy**. This fact forms the foundation of much of the practical considerations in terms of both training methodology and the actual combative Techniques and Tactics. It is, unfortunately, a very poorly understood issue. System 1, because of the incredibly high speeds it runs at, can be better understood as to run on a Probability rather than an Accuracy Algorithm. At blinding speed System 1 makes judgment calls on needed movement patterns (think about a flinch again). It sees an incoming object and it "throws" an arm out in reaction. It is not primarily concerned with accuracy like System 2 is. It is possible to increase accuracy in System 1, but System 1 is not actively seeking accuracy, it is actively seeking survival. Thus it "throws" the arm out in the general direction of the incoming object. System 1 can become more accurate if trained - but even then it may possibly never be perfectly accurate. System 1 also shows a clear regression in accuracy as speed and volume of incoming data increases. So on autopilot System 1 does its best - but its best isn't necessarily perfectly accurate. Once you understand this you will also better understand what we refer to below as the *flailing of the arms*. The *flailing of the arms* is where the CCI has regressed from the initial first accurate attacks to a muddled mess of bodies and limbs that are blindly swinging, moving, falling and/or clinching.

CHALLENGES IN SYSTEM 1

1. **Loss of accuracy in movement patterns**. We explained this above. But as further comment note the following observation: "Speed is an enemy of accuracy and composure — both necessary components of successful attacks." *[de Becker, Gavin; Tom Taylor; Jeff Marquart. Just 2 Seconds (p. 6). Gavin de Becker, Tom Taylor, Jeff Marquart. Kindle Edition.]* De Becker et al. offers this observation after a quantitative analysis of hundreds of successful and unsuccessful assassination attempts. Even though the observation is framed from the position of the attacker - it remains just as relevant for the defender.

2. *Flailing of the arms*. We explained this above.

3. **Fast, "jerky" and explosive movements**. In relation to the Probability Algorithm of System 1, and specifically the speed of System 1's reactions and

movements, System 1's movement patterns are usually very fast and explosive, coming across as almost "jerky" for lack of a better word. The movements frequently explode from one position to the next rather than moving smoothly. This is very observable under controlled conditions. For this reason, there is arguably a lot of sense to develop a training methodology that plays into this dynamic rather than against it. It would necessitate identifying which movement styles and patterns are already ingrained into System 1 and then seeing whether they can be weaponized. Large motor movements play well into this dynamic.

4. **Involuntary movements and reactions**. In a technical sense the reactions aren't completely involuntary, just involuntary in terms of System 2. What is actually happening, as mentioned earlier in the book, System 1 is simply selecting and launching a movement without System 2's consent and much faster than at which System 2 can effectively intervene. It might not complete the whole movement pattern either. System 1 might send the movement and either System 1 or System 2 might halt or recall it. Have you ever noticed how someone getting ready to launch or defend against an attack sometimes twitches involuntarily? Sometimes the twitches can even be quite large. What you are seeing is System 1 actually attacking or defending, but then the movement gets halted or recalled. It's almost like someone that wants to jump off a high diving board, they start the movement but halt the attempt half a step in. This can be the case with someone getting ready to attack; an individual can twitch in the run-up to attack someone. Conversely, a person can be faced with a very hostile individual and when the hostile individual makes a very fast movement in the direction of the attacker - not attacking, just a movement - System 1 launches and recalls a blocking movement which also appears as an involuntary twitch.

5. **Stuckness**. Here we are referring to an individual getting stuck somewhere in an altercation. Let's say he has gained control of an attackers' knife wielding arm - but in the moment the defender doesn't know what to do with it. It essentially is a type of mental freeze happening. It is difficult to say exactly what is happening in the brain here, but we strongly contend it is when System 1 has run out of or can't recall any immediate options. Why we say this is that when we train our clients we teach them to be mindful of when they get stuck and then in that moment to ask themselves what else they can do. This asking of the self is a System 2 function. The moment they do so their brain tends to find options. We start this process out very slow and then speed it up to where it almost seems automatic, however, in this issue of stuckness we don't believe it to be automatic as there is still a moment of prompting the mind for more options.

6. **Fixation on specific elements of the encounter (tunnel vision)**. As System 1 is geared towards survival we frequently find it fixating on the weapons used in an attack. In a knife altercation it locks onto the knife and loses all peripheral awareness of surroundings and the other dynamics present in the CCI. Please note we are not contradicting any other work on the correlations between heart rate, breathing and tunnel vision. We simply believe this fixation is a System 1 issue as it's seemingly involuntary by nature. System 1 chooses on what it wants me to fixate, in System 2 I choose on what I want to fixate.

As a quick note it might seem as if we are vilifying System 1. We are definitely not. System 1, when trained properly, is an unbelievably effective mode of functioning. It's primary strength being its blazing speed. Remember both Klein and Kahneman: System 1's intuitive nature can make complex decisions at rates far surpassing that of System 2. All movement starts in the brain. System 1 selects a movement pattern for you, or in System 2 you select a movement pattern for you. It is only after this selection or decision that movement can happen. Thus, regardless of the System in charge, the movement started in the brain. This begs the question about how well trained your mind is in this regard? Are you able to assess and adapt at high speeds? Is your training specifically developed to enhance this rapid decision making skill? The exciting news is that rapid decision making ability, as well as the other issues with System 1 mentioned above, are highly trainable. For now it's important to absorb this knowledge base as it will consistently be present when we get to the practical sections of this book.

Thus, even if we contend there are some benefits to staying in System 2, we are by no means saying System 1 is not useful. What we are saying is understand System 1's challenges within a CCI and then train for them.

STRATEGIES TO REMAIN IN SYSTEM 2

We will end this chapter with a couple of broad suggestions on how to remain in System 2 for longer. Here are a couple of strategies with which to do so:

BETTER CRITICAL INCIDENT MANAGEMENT MODELS

There are a couple of what we call CIMMs available. In the industries' to which this book relates examples of such models might be Lt. Col. Jeff Cooper's *Awareness Color Code*, Marc MacYoung's *Five Stages of Violent Crime*, The CP

Journal's *Left of Bang*, or Col. John Boyd's **OODA Loop** model. All of these models attempt to give us a framework of some sort through which one can understand how an individual can go through a process of assessing, making decisions about, and re-acting or responding within certain types of incidents. Please note the author's of these models never referred to them as CIMMs, we do, they also did not specifically intend for them to be applied within the scope of this book. However, it is a fact that these models are frequently used within environments related to the scope of this book and we cite them as such.

All of that said, the further ahead we can stay in the development of a critical incident the further away we are from the Switch. If we see an incident developing we might be able to subvert it before any of the Thresholds are crossed. Having a sensible model through which to identify and assess PINs and TDs, make good and effective decisions, and take pro-active action is definitely desirable in this regard. A concise chapter of this book is dedicated to the CIMM that we developed and use. It is called ARM Yourself.

DEVELOP TACTICS THAT ALLOW YOU TO MAINTAIN INITIATIVE

When we have initiative it means that the other is reacting to us. The further away on the timeline we are from the critical incident itself the easier it is to maintain initiative. When we have lost initiative we enter a reactive loop until we regain initiative. Depending on the speed of events this reactive loop might run at a speed in which we will function in System 1. Obviously that means when we retain initiative, we are forcing the other person into a re-active loop, and quite possibly also into System 1. Once we understand the challenges above we can also use them to our advantage. More on this later, for now it is important to understand that maintaining initiative is a key strategy to remaining in System 2 for longer.

FIND HEALING FOR EMOTIONAL TRAUMA

Trauma is not something that happens to you, it is what is left after an event. Getting shot is not trauma, the wound left after getting shot is trauma, as is the emotional damage that is left after such an event. Likewise, the event, whatever it might have been, that has left some form of emotional damage in you wasn't the trauma, the trauma is the actual emotional anchor point that the event has left behind. We, the authors, live in an extremely violent country. Many individuals here have suffered from violence and have been traumatized by it.

Frequently they will come for consultation or training without having resolved this trauma. The trauma influences their reactions and their ability to remain in System 2. We remember one client who was mugged and stabbed decades ago. When she arrived for training she had not found healing for the trauma yet. It greatly retarded her training process, as she would Switch out fear and not danger.

One of the issues we'll be grappling with in the next chapter relates to the following question: If Factors 1& 2 are such a big issue - are there ways that we can better take control of the Switch? Specifically, in the context of Factors 1 & 2, if our senses are the primary pathways through which our brain collects the data, are there senses that are better and worse to rely on? Or rather, are there certain senses that are faster or slower in terms of data collection and transmission? Interestingly we've had very specific and repeatable observations concerning this exact issue. And we can back it up with sensible and repeated research as well. But first, let's focus on the timing of the Switch.

THE MAUL

CHAPTER SIX: ON THE USE OF THE SENSES

LET'S REVISIT THE ISSUE

As noted in the previous chapter, one of the questions we've been grappling with during our research was whether there would be any benefit in relying more or less on certain senses during a CCI. This question arises primarily in response to the Thresholds of Speed and Volume. By clarification, if the incoming data is too fast or too much for System 2 to handle, and System 1 needs to step in, would there be any sense (excuse the pun) to rather rely on one or the other of the body's senses during this process? And asked much, much more practically - is the feedback loop from any one sense, to the brain, and back to the motor unit controlling the muscle fibers that the brain wants to move via the nervous system, faster than any of the others?

And the answer, whether confirmed through our own observational experience and internal research, or corroborated via externally published research, is a resounding yes. In a nutshell, the tactile and auditory senses are faster than the visual sense, tactile also being faster than auditory. So in terms of speed we have tactile on podium position one, auditory on position two, and visual on position three.

If we can just return to the book's introduction quickly recap its essential scope: The Maul, as a system or approach to edge and point use, was developed as a response to certain doubts and questions, as well as the implications of recent research findings on these questions. The primary outcome was to incorporate the findings into training for and performance within CCIs.

Part 2 of this book attempts to frame these research findings as specific problems or guiding principles that we need to seriously consider when selecting and developing Techniques, Tactics and Procedures, as well as their related training methodologies. We mention this for the following reason: whether or not you adopt The Maul as an edge or point system, you need to soberly consider how these findings should and will influence your own training and performance. Thus, feel free to take from these chapters what you need to and incorporate it into your own systems. But we want to encourage you to do the hard work of understanding these chapters well. Do not blindly incorporate the drills or practices in the last part of the book into your training. That said, let's consider the following external research findings.

EXTERNAL RESEARCH

As always, one of the challenges when it comes to academic research is consistency. It always seems like when one looks hard and long enough, it will be possible to find researchers contradicting each others' work. This question of response time related to sensory stimuli is no different. Notice this comparison in findings from an article titled Comparison between Auditory and Visual Simple Reaction Times (Jose Shelton and Gideon Praveen Kumar). Please note that he is comparing visual and auditory alone and bold has been added by us for ease of reading:

Research done by Pain & Hibbs (T. G. Matthew Pain and A. Hibbs, "Sprint Starts and the Minimum Auditory Reaction Time," Journal of Sports Sciences, Vol. 25, No. 1, 2007, pp. 79-86) **shows that simple auditory reaction time has the fastest reaction time for any given stimulus**. *A study done by Thompson et al. (P. D. Thompson, J. G. Colebatch, P. Brown, J. C. Roth-well, B. L. Day and J. A. Obeso, "Voluntary Stimulus Sensitive Jerks and Jumps Mimicking Myoclonus or Pathological Startle Syndromes," Movement Disorders, Vol. 7, No. 3, 1992, pp. 257-262)* **has documented that the mean reaction time to detect visual stimuli is approximately 180 to 200 milliseconds, whereas for sound it is around 140-160 milliseconds.** *On the other hand, there are also researches done by Yagi et al. (Y. Yagi, K. L. Coburn, K. M. Estes and J. E. Arruda, "Effects of Aerobic Exercise and Gender on Visual and Auditory P300, Reaction Time, and Accuracy," European Journal of Applied Physiology, Vol. 80, 1999, pp. 402- 408) that show that reaction time to visual stimuli is faster than to auditory stimuli. Research by Verleger (R. Verlager, "On the Utility of P3 Latency as an Index of Mental Chronometry," Journal of Psychophysiology, Vol. 34, No. 2, 1997, pp. 131-156)* **also confirms that visual reaction time is faster than auditory reaction time during or after exercise**.

So that's two for auditory and two for visual being the fastest. Not helpful is it? Our approach then was the following: First, let's focus on what is found to be agreed upon and then reconcile that with our own observations within CCIs. Next, we will mostly steer away from any gender based findings as they are almost split down the middle depending on which research piece you are reading. Lastly, let's work with the most recent research we can find. In relation to this last point, please note that the research cited by Shelton and Kumar above, specifically the two pieces favoring visual above auditory both date pre 2000. Seeing as this book is being written in 2019, and is primarily concerned with recent research, we can't help but favor articles written within the last decade at least.

All of that said, Shelton and Kumar also provide us with the following notable definitions on Reaction Time (RT) and Simple Reaction Time (SRT). From the same article as cited above, they say:

Reaction time (RT) is the elapsed time between the presentation of a sensory stimulus and the subsequent behavioral response. Simple reaction time is usually defined as the time required for an observer to detect the presence of a stimulus. It is a physical skill closely related to human performance. It represents the level of neuromuscular coordination in which the body through different physical, chemical and mechanical processes decodes visual or auditory stimuli which travel via afferent pathways and reach the brain as sensory stimuli.

On SRT they offer us the following interesting insights:

Reaction time is dependent on several factors like arrival of the stimulus at the sensory organ, conversion of the stimulus by the sensory organ to a neural signal, neural transmissions and processing, muscular activation, soft tissue compliance, and the selection of an external measurement parameter (T. G. Matthew Pain and A. Hibbs, "Sprint Starts and the Minimum Auditory Reaction Time," Journal of Sports Sciences, Vol. 25, No. 1, 2007, pp. 79-86). Researches by Kemp et al. (B. J. Kemp, "Reaction Time of Young and Elderly Subjects in Relation to Perceptual Deprivation and Signal-on Versus Signal-off Condition," Developmental Psychology, Vol. 8, No. 2, 1973, pp. 268-272) show that an auditory stimulus takes only 8-10 milliseconds to reach the brain, but on the other hand, a visual stimulus takes 20-40 milliseconds. This implies that the faster the stimulus reaches the motor cortex, faster will be the reaction time to the stimulus. Therefore since the auditory stimulus reaches the cortex faster than the visual stimulus, the auditory reaction time is faster than the visual reaction time.

Let's borrow the following figure titled Figure 1. Graph showing faster simple reaction time for auditory stimulus compared to visual stimulus from the cited article:

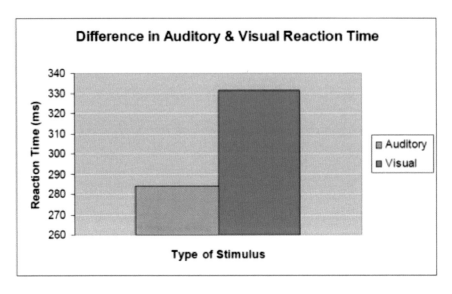

Figure 1. Graph showing faster simple reaction time for auditory stimulus compared to visual stimulus.

Why do we like this specific research piece? First of all, when considered alongside the next article it helps us to understand that there is a definite progression and agreement of findings as research becomes more recent. Meaning, the closer we get to 2019 the more aligned the findings with the following statement: Auditory RT is faster than visual RT. Next, you might notice that some of the research and citations presented in this article are from more physical contexts. Sprinting. Jerks. Jumps. Startle Responses. All of these are definitely more closely related to our field of study than the next article. This does not mean we can easily discount the next article's finding as it's one of the few that sensibly considered the question of tactile stimuli alongside visual and auditory.

In a 2012 published article titled Finger Response Times to Visual, Auditory and Tactile Modality Stimuli (Annie W.Y. Ng and Alan H.S. Chan, Proceedings of the International MultiConference of Engineers and Computer Scientists 2012 Vol II, IMECS 2012, March 14 - 16, 2012 Hong Kong), where 94 right-handed Chinese participants aged 11 to 60 years old, took part in the visual, auditory and tactile stimuli test, it was found that "the response time of tactile stimuli was 28% shorter and 34% shorter than auditory and visual stimuli."

Why do we like this article? The testing mechanism is simple and the research is well controlled. In an extremely simple manner, being devoid of any complex and dynamic CCI context, it tests exactly what we were looking for. Stimuli were delivered via a sensory organ and the action needed in response was as basic and uncomplicated as it gets - a finger that needed to touch a button. Other select interesting findings which should be considered (**quoted directly from the article in bold** and then commented on in regular font):

• **The location of tactile vibrator** (the stimuli for the tactile modality) **i.e. wrist and leg did not have any significant influence on response time**. As we'll discuss later in this chapter one of the other drawbacks of sight is the loss of peripheral vision due to proximity. Tactile stimuli doesn't seem to have this problem - when you feel it you feel it. In some of our drills we work eyes closed, responding to tactile stimuli alone, and, as long as we remain in contact with our opponent, there is no degradation in performance. For this reason, as we start talking about the solution, you will notice a consistent theme of longer contact and/or positive pressure emerging. We want to continually be touching, and never stop touching, our opponents during the CCI.

• **Factors like age, gender, education level, time spent on computer, left/right finger, and choice alternative, however, had significant effects on the response time of an individual to visual and auditory stimuli**. Regardless of what the actual reasons are, it is noted that tactile stimuli response time was not prone to the fluctuations present in visual and auditory stimuli response times.

• **The response of tertiary and secondary education groups was faster than that of primary education group. Besides, the longer the time spent on computer in daily life, the shorter was the response time**. We would venture to glean from this finding that training and/or practice simply and obviously influences our performance.

• **The response on single-choice task was the fastest, followed by two-choice task and then four- and eight-choice tasks**. We add this item simply as proof that more options makes response time slower.

• **The average response time for tactile stimuli was 0.385 ms with standard deviation of 0.071 ms.**

• **The average response time for visual stimuli across all choice tasks and response fingers was 0.517 ms with standard deviation of 0.181 ms.**

• **With regards to auditory stimuli, the average response time across all choice tasks and response fingers was 0.493 ms with standard deviation of 0.178 ms.**

As a last observation on the findings of this article we would like to note that even though all of these response times, meaning visual, auditory and tactile, validly seem to be quite fast (very close to and under half a second), the fact that tactile is 34% faster than visual requires from us a serious reconsideration on how we are gathering data within the CCI. 34% is a third faster. The other obvious question then is whether our training is optimized for gathering data primarily through visual, auditory or tactile stimulus?

INTERNAL OBSERVATIONS AND FINDINGS

As we start this section please note that we are not suggesting that it is wise, or even possible, to function using only one specific sensory organ during a CCI. As repeatedly stated, we are concerned with whether we are training, and can train, ourselves to be more effective under certain conditions. For this reason we need to understand where there are specific limitations related to certain sensory organs and then adapt accordingly. In no particular order our main observations are the following:

• **Proximity creates a definite problem when relying on visual stimulus**. The closer to your opponent you are the less you will be able to see the periphery of their anatomy or actions. If for example, your chin is nestled in his or her neck, it should be obvious that you will not be able to see large parts of what they are doing. You can feel them though. You might not be able to see a limb but you might be able to hold them by or maintain positive pressure against a wrist, forearm or bicep. Thus, apart from sight being slower than touch, under certain conditions sight will simply fail as an effective sensory organ.

• **Auditory exclusion and tunnel vision might be a problem under certain physiological conditions**. Essentially the auditory and visual sides of the same proverbial coin, both of these complications can and usually do arise with certain limbic responses, as well as certain fluctuations in respiratory and heart rate. If and when they do arise, it is obvious that they can negatively influence the reliance on these sensory organs during the CCI. Therefore, it stands to reason that there is much benefit being trained and able to effectively capitalize on the speed and other benefits of the tactile sensory organ.

• **The issue with the probability algorithm**. System 1's probability algorithm, causing large, less accurate, and possibly jerky movements, is directly related to the issue of speed of incoming data. When switching away from the slower visual sensory organ to the faster tactile sensory organ, there is a noticeable increase in RT and the accuracy of our responses. Say for instance I am applying positive pressure with my forearm against my Opponent's forearm, and the Opponent quickly jerks their arm backwards, there is a noticeable difference in both RT and accuracy when simply keeping my forearm against theirs through the positive pressure rather than trying to react using the visual sensory organ. It is our contention that at close range, meaning arm's length and closer, System 1 functions better alongside the tactile sensory organ.

• **The body seems evolved to more naturally and accurately respond to tactile stimulus.** Much of our time has been spent pondering the question of why the tactile sensory organ's RT should be more than a third faster than the auditory and visual sensory organs. Our conclusion is that it relates to the proximity of risk or threats. Essentially, on open ground, we can see further in the day than what we can frequently hear and most obviously touch. In dark or enclosed spaces (houses, towns, jungles, forests) we can see significantly less further than what we can potentially hear and possibly touch. Hearing then needs to be faster for survival purposes. If I can hear a threat then it means that the threat is close and that there is a higher possibility of risk than if could see a threat further away. Following this line of thought it becomes clear that if I can touch the threat, or if the threat can touch me, it is obviously close enough to be an immediate danger to me. Tracing this argument backwards then, to us, it makes sense that our fastest reaction time should be related to the tactile sensory organ as it literally means a potentially higher survival rate.

As a last note we want to mention that we understand the immense benefit of adding the olfactory sensory organ to our larger contextual toolbox. This book being focused specifically on the CCI it should make sense why sight, hearing and touch are our primary areas of focus.

THE MAUL

<u>CHAPTER SEVEN: SHORT NOTE ON TIME FRAMES</u>

It is important to acknowledge that positioning, the art of an Opponent placing themselves in range for an attack, has a very large influence on the time frames involved during critical incidents. Positioning has to happen, and it happens right before an attack is launched. The Opponent positions simply because all weapons have effective ranges. That is, for the threat of violence to be valid, the Opponent has to be within a range from which he or she can successfully execute the threat. This range is determined by the weapon involved. This should make it clear why we state that positioning influences the time frames of an incident. However, for the purpose of this chapter, we are going to leave positioning, as well as its influence on the time frame aside, and focus purely on what we can learn concerning durations of certain types of attacks, or rather, in the parlance of this book, the durations of the actual CCIs. That said; let's have a quick look at existing research on the time frames of CCIs:

ON ASSASSINATION ATTEMPTS

In *Just 2 Seconds*, de Becker et al, sheds much light on the understanding of time frames after researching hundreds of successful and unsuccessful assassination attempts. Momentarily disregarding weapon platforms and the context of the attacks, they provide us with the following chilling insight:

The extensive study undertaken for this book has produced many insights, the most striking of which is also the simplest: From the Moment of Commitment onward, the overwhelming majority of public figure attacks are over in less than five seconds. Within just those few seconds, all the damage that will be done has been done. [de Becker, Gavin; Tom Taylor; Jeff Marquart. Just 2 Seconds (p. 5). Gavin de Becker, Tom Taylor, Jeff Marquart. Kindle Edition.]

Five seconds is the time it takes for most readers to finish this sentence.

Read that again.

In de Becker et al's findings on specifically assassinations attempts 5 seconds was the time in which the majority of CCIs were resolved.

ON KNIFE ATTACKS

In 2016, after studying over 150 knife attacks, Patrice Bonnafoux released an article *[Self-defense against knife attacks: evidence-based approach. Patrice Bonnafoux.]* detailing his findings. Key excerpts pertaining to the time frames of knife attacks are as follows:

• There's a peak in the number of attacks around 7 seconds with 25.2% of all attacks lasting between 5 and 10 seconds, and half of all attacks lasting 14 seconds or less.

• The average incident time (i.e. arithmetic mean) for knife attacks, from the moment the attack is launched to the moment it stops, is 23 seconds.

• But 80% of all attacks last less than 32 seconds:

We frequently run a drill in our training events where we have one Trainee prepare to be stabbed with a training knife. Another individual has a timer and times 2 seconds verbally and out loud. Another individual has to count the amount of stabs landed by the Opponent. We have run this drill hundreds of times and we always land between 7 - 11 stabs. Note that this is on a Trainee that knows the attack is coming, when it will start, as well as which area of his or her body it will be aimed at.

Observations from Don Pentecost, who worked and wrote his book, *Put 'Em Down. Take 'Em Out!: Knife Fighting Techniques From Folsom Prison* within the American penal system, confirms the general thrust of all of these observations:

The time frame of a knife attack is usually very short - it is often over in a matter of seconds.

THE ISSUE OF TIME

We would like to impress upon you the extremely short time frames of CCIs. They literally span seconds.

This reality should help you further understand that your brain is most probably going to have to switch to System 1 to deal with the event. Any training that you develop and partake in then should be geared towards functioning effectively within these short time frames, and as such, within System 1. Also, all Techniques, Tactics and Procedures should be chosen and further developed to function specifically within these short time frames. What does this mean practically?

That your training methods must:

1. Be able to identify and intercept an incoming attack in such a way that you don't get critically injured,

2. Gain control of the dynamic altercation long enough to regain initiative,

3. Counter attack in such a way that you can stop the attack if not immediately then very soon,

4. All in a timeframe of somewhere roughly between 5 to 32 seconds for a very large percentage of attacks.

Which again begs the question concerning what you are training for and what you are fit for. If your training is not geared towards providing the above capability within the mentioned time frames we want to kindly suggest that you re-evaluate your current methods or approach. We also say this not from a tribalist point of view, as if what we do and how we do it is the perfect approach, but from a sincere position of care. Whether you simply draw from the drills we developed, adopt The Maul completely, or simply adapt your existing methodologies, you must ensure that you develop these specific capabilities.

THE MAUL

CHAPTER EIGHT: IMPLICATIONS ON TRAINING METHODOLOGIES

In this chapter we are going to condense the previous chapters under a couple of easy to remember headings and principles. These principles are applicable to all forms of CCI training and not just to The Maul as featured later in the book. The Maul is simply how we packaged them into an edge and point system. It is definitely recommended to study the previous chapters well in order to incorporate that knowledge thoroughly into your foundation, but sometimes we need a quick reference on the practical implications of what we've learned. This chapter will hopefully provide that reference.

ALWAYS REMEMBER THE NATURE OF VIOLENCE

Just to recap, we stated the Nature of Violence consists of three fundamental tenets. Violence is

• Inherently complex,

• Extremely dynamic,

• And as such, has an unpredictable outcome.

The first two tenets are the key to developing sensible training methodologies. The first two tenets combined lead to the third, meaning: *Inherently Complex + Extremely Dynamic = Unpredictable Outcome*. For this reason we say the first two are the key.

On a practical level it means that both your training environment as well as your training simulations should contain both complexity as well as dynamic elements. To further clarify, here are some thoughts on those two elements. The list below is not comprehensive, rather, it's purpose is to stimulate your own thinking and development. Context and outcome would strongly influence these elements and how they might change. Therefore, as a good instructor or Trainee, you need to address the questions on what types of complexity and dynamism your context includes and then adapt your training methodologies accordingly.

INHERENTLY COMPLEX

1. Ideas on background and training.

    1.1. Use different movement patterns in the Opponents, both in terms of general movement and lines or patterns of attack.

    1.2. Change between left and right handedness in the Opponent.

    1.3. Play around with state of mind.

    1.4. Play around with the Opponent's movement and attack speed.

    1.5. Attempt to simulate different attitudes or emotional energies in the opponent.

2. Ideas on motivation.

    2.1. Create different points of disengagement for the Opponents.

    2.2. Create fluctuating levels of motivation for the Opponents.

EXTREMELY DYNAMIC

1. Ideas for environmental changes.

    1.1. Vary the venue or layout of the training environment.

    1.2. Leave varying equipment randomly scattered on training floor.

    1.3. Change the lighting in the training environment.

2. Ideas on situational changes.

    2.1. Randomly introduce extra participants during training.

    2.2. Have multiple potential Opponents without prior indication on who's the confirmed threat.

2.3. If working in a stack facilitate the point man (or any other member in the stack) going to the floor during an entry.

2.4. Simulate loss of use of a limb.

2.5. Change the starting position of the Trainee.

3. Ideas on Internal Changes.

3.1. Develop methods to induce fear, agitation, panic etc. in the Trainee.

3.2. Occasionally use overwhelming force (not damage) on the Trainee.

3.3. Interject exercises into the training process to facilitate a change in heart and respiratory rate.

3.4. Develop methods to induce tunnel vision and auditory exclusion.

None of the above is listed or meant as cliché reality based training of any kind. There is no need to over exaggerate any of the elements or ideas listed. The bottom line is that recognition and movement run to the brain and from the brain respectively. Therefore we always say movement starts in the brain. If you do not expose the brain regularly to different stimulus it will never learn to select and execute appropriate solutions.

The skill in good training development is to ensure that a Trainee can first execute well under regular controlled conditions before adding any of the ideas from above. Training processes thus should provide for both controlled conditions as well as unscripted conditions. It's important to understand the risks involved with any of the above ideas and to adequately control for these risks as well as be able to mitigate any injury or other fallout arising from the use of the above ideas.

USE SYSTEM 2 TO TRAIN SYSTEM 1

System 2 has some ability to change the way System 1 works, by programming the normally automatic functions of attention and memory.[Kahneman, Daniel. Thinking, Fast and Slow (p. 21-22). Penguin Books Ltd. Kindle Edition.]

A crucial capability of System 2 is the adoption of "task sets": it can program memory to obey an instruction that overrides habitual responses. [Kahneman, Daniel. Thinking, Fast and Slow (p. 36). Penguin Books Ltd. Kindle Edition.]

System 1 is trainable. It does, however, require specific approaches in terms of how we train it. Risking oversimplification for the goal of easy understanding, let's approach the topic from what we learned in the chapter on The Switch. System 1 is like an autopilot. It runs off preprogrammed algorithms, movement patterns, reactions and responses. We learned that one of the primary factors involved in the brain's switching to System 1 is speed of incoming data. System 1 is significantly better equipped to deal with very high speeds of incoming data. In System 2 I am actively thinking and in System 1 thinking is happening, in the context of this book, primarily due to the issues related to speed.

We can consistently show that there is a speed Threshold under which the autopilot of System 1 becomes active and as such, when we cross that Threshold, certain types of learning cannot take place. Sticking to the analogy of an autopilot, whilst autopilot is piloting it cannot be reprogrammed. That said though, our brain's are highly adept at learning through any life saving action. As such if something worked whilst in System 1 there is a good chance your brain will retain it. However, for the treatment of this book, being focused on the development of training methodologies, that is not the only or primary form of learning we are interested in. Also, in terms of this specific principle, we are focused on the question of how do we implant new algorithms, movement patterns, reactions and responses into System 1, i.e. how do we program and reprogram System 1?

If we have to bring all of this together we can safely say that to effectively train System 1 we need to be training at speeds where System 2 can remain in charge. We have an adage in training:

Don't train faster than which you can think. Speed will come.

See this interesting note from Kahneman:

One of the main functions of System 2 is to monitor and control thoughts and actions "suggested" by System 1, allowing some to be expressed directly in behavior and suppressing or modifying others. [Kahneman, Daniel. Thinking, Fast and Slow (p. 44). Penguin Books Ltd. Kindle Edition.]

Our training speeds, specifically related to implanting new algorithms, movement patterns, reactions and responses into System 1, therefore need to be at a speed where System 2 can *still actively monitor and control thoughts and actions "suggested" by System 1*. If we continue to do so System 1 will eventually learn and our speed of execution will increase naturally.

LET SYSTEM 1 DO WHAT IT DOES BEST

The previous principle engaged the issue of how do we implant new algorithms, movement patterns, reactions and responses. This principle builds on top of that and assumes that we have achieved a certain level of success in implanting effective options into System 1; this principle pertains primarily to the conditioning of System 1 through experience. So if we could sketch a rough process to better illustrate what we mean by this it would look like the following:

1. Identify effective algorithms, movement patterns, reactions and responses.

2. Train them slow and controlled under System 2.

3. Speed training up periodically to test how effectively System 1 has been trained.

4. Either identify the required level of consistency in terms of correct execution and move on, or revert back to steps 2 and 3.

5. Add elements of complexity and dynamism, Unscripted Training as well as Play Learning (more on these two elements later in the chapter), and allow System 1 to further condition itself.

Gary Klein offers the following insight that'll also help us to grapple with this issue:

Intuitive judgments reflect the experiences we've had and can help us respond quickly to situations. They are sensitive to context and nuance, letting us read situations and also read other people. We can make successful decisions without using analytical methods, but we cannot make good decisions without drawing on our intuitions. Yet our intuitions aren't foolproof, and we always have to worry that they are going to mislead us. [Klein, Gary. Streetlights and Shadows: Searching for the Keys to Adaptive Decision Making (MIT Press) (p. 80). The MIT Press. Kindle Edition.]

What we are essentially trying to do through effective training is to create experience. Experience that mimics the demands that will be placed on the brain in actual critical incidents. This experience, when accurate, then allows System 1 to make better intuitive judgments. It allows us to make successful decisions at speeds surpassing those of System 2. It will also drive movement reactions and responses at much higher speeds than System 2 can, but we need to ensure, as best we can, that the algorithms, movement patterns, reactions and responses which we implant into System 1 has been developed specifically to be effective whilst operating in and from System 1. System 1 will then be able to make high speed selections from those options and be significantly more effective than System 2 under most CCI conditions.

In complex settings in which we have to take the context into account, we can't codify all the work in a set of procedures. No matter how comprehensive the procedures, people probably will run into something unexpected and will have to use their judgment. [Klein, Gary. Streetlights and Shadows: Searching for the Keys to Adaptive Decision Making (MIT Press) (p. 19). The MIT Press. Kindle Edition.]

In our training environments then, we teach algorithms, movement patterns, reactions and responses in the form of AOPs, Techniques, Tactics and Procedures. We do this as a basis of understanding, but the goal is to move past them as fast as possible. As fast as possible means as fast as the Trainee can execute correctly. Correct Execution needs to always determine training speed. As speed of execution develops training speed can increase accordingly. We want to let System 1 do what it does best. However, we need to develop training methodologies that nurture these dynamics.

Let's wrap up with a final quote from Klein:

Procedures are most useful in well-ordered situations when they can substitute for skill, not augment it. In complex situations— in the shadows— procedures are less likely to substitute for expertise and may even stifle its development. Here is a different statement that I think works better: In complex situations, people will need judgment skills to follow procedures effectively and to go beyond them when necessary. [Klein, Gary. Streetlights and Shadows: Searching for the Keys to Adaptive Decision Making (MIT Press) (p. 28). The MIT Press. Kindle Edition.]

TRAIN CONTINUOUS ASSESSMENT HABITS INTO SYSTEM 1

One of the primary lacks we encounter in training environments is the algorithm of Continuous Assessment. This is primarily due to the fact that most training environments, especially commercial and low quality professional environments, are scripted by design. The trainee is pre-inducted in exactly what will be trained before training commences. In layman's terms, the trainee already knows what is coming. If the training methodology does not require the trainee to Continuously Assess, then the trainee's brain will never develop the discipline to Continuously Assess. Therefore, we need to ask where and how do we bring Continuous Assessment into our training environments.

Why is Continuous Assessment important though? Due to the nature of violence being extremely dynamic. The CCI will always be changing, and doing so at high speeds. This necessitates the ability and discipline to stay in touch with those changes as they happen. It requires a strong discipline of Continuous Assessment. Here are three training strategies which might aid in the development of this discipline:

1. **Initial assessment**. Never start a combative response before having completed an assessment. This strategy presupposes that the trainee has been educated in terms of both Pre-Incident iNdicators (PINs) as well as Tactic Determinants (TDs).

2. **Include training sections with slow assessment and selection loops**. Create training drills where the speed is slow enough that the Trainee can loop the mental process of assessment and selection of appropriate responses as they are working. As a training aid you can let the trainees literally ask themselves two things out loud: What is happening? And, What is the best course of action? When answering the question What is happening? they need to be able to address both Current Reality as well as any TDs.

3. **Stuck assessment**. Any time an individual trainee freezes or gets stuck have the working group freeze, not disengage. Be aware that most trainees will disengage when you say stop. You need to teach them to freeze in position and not to disengage. When they have frozen, have the stuck individual do an assessment of the situation again, it might very well help to let them ask the assessment question out loud as this ensures that they are in System 2. After the assessment let them ask themselves what options they have and which might be the best course of action. This is also a phenomenal teaching aid for the instructor as the instructor can provide guidance in the form of new or better solutions within actual and realistic sticking points. After a response has been selected let them continue.

MINIMALIZE FIXED PATTERNS AND COMBINATIONS

 In our experience fixed patterns or combinations work best when you lead with them, i.e. before the Switch and the *flailing of the arms* start. It's also our contention that they are best launched from System 2 as this will assist greatly with accuracy. This means there should be a balance between leading with a fixed pattern or combination and switching over to a more dynamic and free-wheeling approach. Training should facilitate both these sides of the coin, purposefully creating spaces where you are required to switch back and forth between them.

In the Maul (our edge and point system), our training is structured as follows:

1. **Train for specific scenarios**. Here we are very careful not to train for types of attacks but rather types of events or tactical situations. This would be the difference between learning a defense for an ice pick stab versus simulating the initial stages of a mugging, or on the tactical side, having to close distance to affect a takedown for arrest.

2. **Select combinations that work well whilst we have initiative**. Combinations are goal specific (see below) and need to have a specific purpose within the scenario. At best the combination should either end the incident (accomplish the goal) or at least put your opponent under enough pressure to force them into a reactive loop whilst you switch over to System 1.

3. **Have less than three moves to the combination**. It is very infrequent that these combinations have more than three movements in them. Sometimes a single technique, executed accurately and with enough force, is enough to accomplish the goal, other times you will need to stack it with one or two other techniques. The challenge with having too many techniques is twofold. One, we might regress into the flailing of the arms and run into the accuracy issues, and two, your opponent's brain will at least have picked up something is happening and started to move reactively. His movements might be clumsy, messy and uncoordinated, or they may be extremely coordinated and effective. Regardless of which, the situation for which you launched the combination has now changed and as such the combination will probably lack effectiveness.

SWITCH FROM TECHNIQUE HEAVY TO GOAL DRIVEN

Training that matches the real thing helps. Differences in expectation and reality create glitches. Glitches freeze you. Nothing works every time so you must practice recovering from failure. The Threat chooses the time and place so you must practice working from positions of disadvantage. [Miller, Rory. Facing Violence: Preparing for the Unexpected (Kindle Locations 2695-2697). YMAA Publication Center. Kindle Edition.]

One of the ways we relate with the idea of "differences in expectation and reality create glitches," is in terms of techniques that were developed to counter very specific movement patterns.

Think all of the different knife counters and disarms in the Krav Maga or reality based self defense systems. Defense against ice pick attack, defense against upward stab, defense against slashes, defense against straight stabs etc., the list is honestly never ending. There are two problems with this. Firstly, it is seldom that movement patterns, especially in a dynamic violent encounter, are very neat, tidy, uniform or singular. Angles and planes of movement are especially dynamic in close combat. This means that if you are training specific angles, your brain will be primed for them. If your brain is primed for a specific angle and the angle changes you'll experience a glitch. And secondly, the initial phases of an attack are very similar in terms of your opponent's body movements. It is our experience and very strong contention that if you had to pick a technique based defensive response AFTER an assault has been launched, and the Opponent doesn't launch what was expected, your brain will experience a glitch and simply Switch to System 1's auto pilot (which might or might not be effective in that incident).

As an example from our own training consider the following. We never graded in our training. We developed what we called *test night*. At *test night,* everyone gets attacked as randomly as we could engineer. Weapons were random, amount of attackers were random, whether a specific person in play would attack or not was random, apart from the fact that you knew that someone was going to attack you (and not necessarily who), everything else was controlled to be as random as possible. There was one referee and multiple students assisting with safety control and until the referee called it you had to continue the encounter. For every attack you either scored a 1 or a 0, i.e. you made it or you didn't. After your fight we debrief. At the end of *test night* the group debriefs. Everyone is attacked 20 times during *test night* and you have a score by the end of the night. Our work as instructors was to make sure that over the duration of your training that the score progressively increased.

Now here's the kicker.

When we first launched *test night*, most of our clients would get stuck mid fight. Afterwards when debriefing they would simply state "they couldn't remember what to do." That simple but extremely telling statement is partly what drove this book's research. Why would clients that trained for quite a while still not remember what to do in a dynamic encounter? One of the reasons was the reality that our training was technique heavy. Listen closely, the Techniques were not the problem, the training methodology was. We were teaching our clients Techniques - not how to fight. This experience was a wakeup call and we felt led to seriously reconsider our training methods.

One of the biggest changes born out of this revelation was that we moved over to a goal-driven approach. We then changed the structure of our training sessions and developed new training methods to facilitate this goal-driven approach.

The five goals we usually work with are as follows:

1. Assess.

2. Enter.

3. Control.

4. Takedown (or Release in other contexts).

5. Finish.

Thinking about this quote from Klein:

Procedures are typically just a series of "if-then" rules. In following procedures, we perform each step until we reach the criterion that tells us that we have finished that step and should start the next one. When we see these steps and the cues and criteria for starting and completing each step, the process looks straightforward. The challenge lies in judging whether the criteria have been met. Is it time to start the next step, or not? [Klein, Gary. Streetlights and Shadows: Searching for the Keys to Adaptive Decision Making (MIT Press) (p. 39). The MIT Press. Kindle Edition.]

When we (the authors of this book) provide training, we essentially teach Trainees how to work through a step (or goal in our terminology), and how to and when to transition to a next goal. We also work very strongly on the following idea:

Your first fight is for Control, your second fight is to Finish.

There is a whole chapter of the book assigned to this process in Part 4 and we will attend to the details there.

TECHNIQUES SHOULD FUNCTION WELL IN SYSTEM 1

When selecting Techniques to ingrain into System 1, especially when it comes to the CCI context, we want to make sure they check certain boxes. These boxes relate specifically to the issues discussed in the chapters on The Switch and the Senses. Here is a concise list of checks we use, the more of these tests a Technique passes the easier we will consider it:

1. **Working with and from very instinctive movements like the flinch and duck should be accepted**. There are commercial close combat systems that propose that the flinch and duck can be untrained and replaced with other movements. It is our strong contention that this is not possible. We have tried to do so, we have tested the efficacy of these attempts in multiple contexts over at least a decade and have come to the conclusion that it is not possible. If you are operating in a pro-active manner, meaning you have made a decision on a course of action and you are now actively pushing forward, shooting in for an interception or entry, or doing whatever other form or manner of pro-actively movement to address the problem, the odds are that you will avoid flinching or ducking. However, if you are caught unaware, whether an attack didn't originate within your field of view, or whether the incoming data was simply too fast or too much, there is an extremely high probability that System 1 will flinch or duck. This should be accepted and embraced. The speed at which System 1 achieves these flinches and ducks are significantly higher than anything you can generate out of System 2. It is an evolutionary survival response. Rather than trying to untrain it - incorporate it. Train from it, i.e. simulate a flinch and a duck and train transitioning from that into your desired next step.

2. **Techniques should be just as comfortable working explosively offensively as well as reactionary defensively**. Although our goal is to train System 1 to high levels of accuracy, the reality is that when we have time, System 2 will always remain more apt towards planned and well aimed (therefore more accurate) movements. Think about the seemingly simple concept of shoving someone on the chest. If in System 2, and assuming we have enough to time to plan and prepare for the movement, we might follow a similar process as the one described

under the heading System 2 below. Note first of all that these bullet points are extremely concise - but there is still a lot happening in each. Then note how System 1 shortcuts the steps.

2.1. System 2:

    2.1.1.   We would make the decision to shove the person.

    2.1.2.   We can now range perfectly and base our feet properly in preparation.

    2.1.3.   On top of this we can direct our bodies to assume a position that might be most effective for the shove.

    2.1.4.   We can start and execute the shove with good body movement generating the most amount of power possible.

2.2. System 1:

    2.2.1.   We would not be making the decision from System 2, System 1's autopilot would be directing and making the decision for us.

    2.2.2.   As System 1 predominantly cares about addressing problems immediately there is an extremely high likelihood that it would launch the shove from whatever range and base the body is currently in.

    2.2.3.   Because System 1 has taken a shortcut through points 2.1.2. and 2.1.3. above, the shove is compromised and will struggle to hit the perfect target or generate the power desired.

Bear in mind, this example just highlights the difference in execution between the two Systems. Let's now apply this quick example to the point in question. When we understand the differences in how the two Systems influence our execution, we can let that understanding guide our Technique selection. It will probably not be possible to select techniques that function perfectly within both Systems, but we can at least consider whether a Technique would have a sensible application and good execution in both Systems. In our experience,

Techniques that solve this dual application problem can be used offensively in an explosive striking manner, but also offer protection in the form of blocking and deflection when you are caught off guard.

3. **Techniques should provide for longer contact or positive pressure should it be required**. The issue at hand here relates to the specific Tactics that we use. Thinking back to the goals that we are trying to achieve, both Control and the ability to affect a Takedown are reliant on our ability to first attach ourselves to the Opponent. For this reason we want to use techniques that provide for slightly longer contact or positive pressure so that we can turn this initial contact or pressure into a form of stabilized Control. It is important to note that the timeframes here are extremely small. This process happens blindingly fast and its progression is frequently missed - but it is there. As a practical example consider two options:

3.1. The opponent strikes out, I want to Control the striking arm. I block.

    3.1.1. The block might be effective. It might not be. Either way, after the strike and block both trainee and opponent retracts and continues to a second movement pattern. Strikes and blocks have an automatic piston action. They shoot out to come back. That out and back movement pattern is preprogrammed into System 1. Thus, and this is important, there is no option in the brain to grab the striking limb at the end of the initial blocking pattern. The brain does not see the out and back piston action of the block as two separate movements into which it can interject a grab. Neither does the Opponent's brain see the out and back action of the strike as two separate movements - meaning the Opponent will automatically retract the strike and not leave it extended where it is at risk to be grabbed.

3.2. The opponent strikes out, I want to Control the striking arm. I Trap.

    3.3. We'll discuss Trapping as a Technique later in the book. But with the Trap System 1 is tasked to slightly deflect the strike but to maintain contact for a couple of moments. This means the brain now has options at the end of that movement pattern. It could grab or it could retract. Because the longer contact, that positive pressure, is a tactile option (think back to the senses) the brain is actually able to respond faster than what it would have using sight. The feedback is much more immediate seeing as the trainee can now feel what the opponent is doing and better respond. It still doesn't mean the Opponent will leave the striking limb out there, but if an opportunity presents itself, it will be that slightly longer contact and positive pressure that gives us the ability to grab.

4. **Techniques should have small and tight arcs and short patterns of movement.** Referring back to an issue highlighted in point 3 above, we need to always remember that movements start in the brain. In terms of movement, the brain issues a command that has both a start and an end position. It can only launch a next movement after that initial movement has reached its end. For example, if I tell you to hang your arm at your side and to lift it all the way to the top, there would be a start and an end position in the movement arc. Whilst in System 2 I can tell you to lift the arm, and then halfway tell you to change direction to forward instead of up. In System 2 you are able to do this because you are moving slower than what you can think. Thus System 2 can change the direction willfully. However, in System 1 those starts and ends are preselected and also running on a probability algorithm. System 1 does an educated guess on where it thinks the arm should go and it usually just starts from wherever it is. It's not wired to suddenly change that movement pattern, instead it layers movement patterns on top of one another. It acts like a list that it wants to execute, the items on the list being completed movement patterns. This should be a glaring problem to anyone interested in increasing performance at high speeds. Whether the issue at hand is the use of your legs or that of your arms, if you are making very long and wide arcs of movement it means you can only redeploy that leg or arm at the end of the arc. Unfortunately we haven't found a way to retrain System 1 in this manner. But we have created a hack by only working with small and tight arcs and patterns of movement. Having two small movements instead of one long movement means System 1 can now affect one extra direction change during that micro phase of the CCI. And in our books, that adaptability is extremely important in any CCI.

5. **Techniques should be comfortable working from a regular walking stride and not require complicated stance transitions.** This point relates to two issues. The first is point 4 above. If we are taking very long steps or transitioning through very wide stances it means that we lose adaptability during the step or transition. Think about it in this way

to ease remembering: You will be able to use a leg most effectively when, one, on the floor and two, if using it won't create a balance problem. Tighter steps mean that your feet will be on the floor more frequently and that you won't have the risk of developing a balance issue. The second issue relates to the fact that we are not preparing for controlled or sport fighting environments. If System 1 needs to hijack the body for survival it will do so as soon as the Switch happens, the Switch however might happen from any body position, but simple odds are it will happen from whatever position your body finds itself in predominantly. For most of us, that position is a slightly staggered stance or a walking stride. Therefore we highly emphasize techniques that can be safely and effectively launched from a walking stride and we avoid any techniques requiring wide or abnormal stances, as well as those that require complicated transitions for initial power generation.

6. **Techniques should be selected and deployed primarily to stop an attack immediately.** Essentially there are only three ways of immediately stopping another human being. A massive drop in blood pressure, severing or severely disrupting the CNS, or removing its base (think breaking or removing a leg, loss of balance). We strongly contend that Techniques selected and deployed should be graded as primary and secondary in the following manner:

   6.1. **Primary Techniques.** Primary Techniques would be all Techniques that fit the above description, but adjusted to context and outcome. These Techniques should be able to facilitate these three methods as fast as possible whilst still adhering to other principles listed in this chapter. The goal of primary Techniques are then to stop the actual attack as fast a possible with as few movements as possible.

   6.2. **Secondary Techniques.** Secondary Techniques would be any technique we use to assist us in preparing an opponent for deployment of, or compliance to, a primary Technique. As above, all Techniques selected should be adjusted for context and outcome. In other terms we might say we use these terms to "soften up" the opponent, although, we are not "softening up" just for the sake of doing so. We are "softening up" so that we can finish the opponent off.

7. **Weapons or movement patterns should NOT require small or extremely accurate target acquisition to be successful**. The issue at hand here is to try and increase our odds of connecting and creating damage. This is important because of the fact that System 1, due to its inherent probability algorithm, loses a certain amount of accuracy after the speed threshold is crossed. In terms of our body's own weapons we favor larger surface weapons above smaller surface weapons. For hand to hand this could mean favoring elbows and forearms, for example, above fists or fingers. We might use fingers to the eyes, but it would only be in a situation where the hands are already on the face providing longer contact. In terms of edged and pointed weapons, say for instance a pikal style blade, we would create a longer contact time through altering the movement pattern; instead of simply deploying a plain stab we would purposefully drag or rip the blade at the end of the movement pattern giving us a higher probability of connecting, and as such, of creating damage.

If you already prescribe to an existing close combat system it might seem futile or daunting to check your Techniques, Tactics and Procedures against this list but it is our contention it would be highly beneficial to do so. It will free up a lot of your time to work on situational and experiential methodologies. Why? Because once you adopt this approach you will find that your list of Techniques will shrink.

Unfortunately, we also know that if you are in a commercial enterprise this shrinkage of effective Techniques might very well create insecurity for you as it technically means that you are keeping your clients busy with unnecessary content. That is okay if your client is training with you for fitness, arts or sports. If however, they are training with you for self defense, or any form of operational necessity, it is a point of integrity whether you are wasting their time with content that isn't necessary in general, and less effective in System 1 specifically.

INCREASE THE VOLUME OF UNSCRIPTED TRAINING

With experience we learn to see things that others don't notice. [Klein, Gary. Streetlights and Shadows: Searching for the Keys to Adaptive Decision Making (MIT Press) (p. 36). The MIT Press. Kindle Edition.]

The more we get exposed to differences and fluctuations in our training environments the better we will be able to react and respond to them in an actual CCI. With differences and fluctuations we do not refer to novelty for novelty's sake. We refer to different styles and types of attacks and defenses, different tactics, different movement speeds, patterns and angles of attack and so forth. When we (the authors) teach others how to deal with an incoming knife attack we expose them to different angles of attack from the first lesson.

Consider the following thoughts by Klein:

Every type of expert we have studied has built up a repertoire of patterns to quickly make sense of what is happening. These patterns aren't facts, or rules, or procedures. They are based on all the experiences and events the experts have lived through and heard about. They are the basis of intuitions. [Klein, Gary. Streetlights and Shadows: Searching for the Keys to Adaptive Decision Making (MIT Press) (p. 41). The MIT Press. Kindle Edition.]

For these reasons we don't follow a model of one session for this type or another session for that type of attack in our training. If we have been true to the other principles in this chapter it means that the Techniques we use should be effective over a wide range of applications. Better then to start applying that Technique to various problems as fast as the Trainee is able to do so whilst maintaining Correct Execution.

If we find the trainee struggling to remain consistent it then means that the programming of System 1 needs more work. In this case we lean back from Unscripted Training opting to practice the Technique more in a controlled environment, and then switching back to Unscripted as soon as everyone feels comfortable trying it again. This method of switching to and fro between controlled and Unscripted Training allows two methods of learning to take place: Slow and controlled programming through System 2 based training and practice, and an experience based conditioning coming from System 1 successfully applying the technique in an Unscripted environment. It also allows the instructor insight into how well the Techniques are really ingrained into System 1. Always remember that Correct Execution means the trainee achieves a specific desired outcome with the Technique, not simply a perfectly mimicked movement.

CREATE SPACE FOR PLAY LEARNING

When we observe animal or human infants we notice how frequently they play fight. These play fights are very natural and organic and usually contain two types of movement patterns: Those observed from the community and then mimicked, and those that the body naturally wants to do, i.e. it lacks the complexity of fancy and intricate movement patterns. As they play however they are learning lessons about "what works" and what simply doesn't. The play environment has no real controls other than the set of intra-species social rules governing base behavior. What we mean by this, is that the participants tacitly understand they shouldn't severely hurt or injure the other. Apart from that though, most things go.

What is the difference between Play Learning and Unscripted Training?

In Unscripted Training we will still have a focus on a specific Technique or Procedure, but we won't completely script the opponent's role. For example, in the context of this book, we might be training accessing a fixed blade with only one hand. With scripted training we would predetermine a situation and movement pattern in the Opponent (for example the Opponent is rushing you), the Trainee would then practice accessing within that script. In Unscripted Training the situation and movement patterns of the Opponent are the Opponents choice and the Trainee is not informed about it. The Trainee now needs to deploy the Technique successfully in response to the consistently changing stimulus the Opponent provides.

Play Learning differs in the fact that there is no specific focus on a Technique or Procedure. We might determine a very basic outcome, like disengage, escape, defend, arrest, kill etc (and maybe not even that), as well as a starting position, and then we let the participants work the CCI out for themselves. Our main control is that we manage the speed of the session as there is a propensity to speed up and this creates risk and also halters the learning experience.

The main benefits in Play Learning are as follows:

1. **It more easily coaxes out departures from existing Tactics and Procedures than scripted or Unscripted Training**. These departures, not necessarily being positive/effective or negative/ ineffective, create powerful learning opportunities. One of the predominant questions in any departure would be "why did you choose to do that?" It also allows an opportunity for more experienced instructors and Trainees to give input to others because when they do deviate, it is usually because they tacitly know the deviation is going to be more effective.

2. **It conditions System 1 faster than other methods**. As discussed previously, the brain is extremely adept at accepting any response that ensures survival. Thus, in Play Learning, System 1 can better see what is working and what not. It

also allows the formation of personal style and strategy. Always remember that biomechanics, speed, physiology, age, gender and many more variables, influences the Trainee's actual capabilities. These variables in our Opponent's again should influence our Tactics. When we develop a style, we are adopting methods that play better into our unique advantages and disadvantages, as well as Tactics that are better suited against the unique attributes of our Opponents. Play Learning allows this style to develop significantly faster than other methods of learning.

3. **Lastly, from an instructor point of view, you can learn two other important things**: First, Play Learning will give you very good insight into how well System 1 has been trained, and secondly, if there are Trainees who have a very high aptitude to successfully navigate a CCI, it will show up best in Play Learning. How will it show? That Trainee will display high levels of adaptability and creativity, they will achieve the set outcome faster and with fewer movements than the others, and they will Correctly Execute Techniques and Procedures they have been trained in (i.e. they assimilate training better than others).

In relation to departures from existing Procedures Gary Klein makes a similar observation:

It is hard to give people feedback about tacit knowledge. As a result, when settings or tasks are complex we give feedback about departures from procedures instead of helping people to notice subtle cues and patterns. [Klein, Gary. Streetlights and Shadows: Searching for the Keys to Adaptive Decision Making (MIT Press) (p. 45). The MIT Press. Kindle Edition.]

TIMEFRAMES - MOBILITY, BREATHING AND ENERGY SYSTEMS

As we discussed in the chapter on Timeframes, there are definite guidelines in terms of what can be expected in a CCI specifically. In this context we are specifically talking about the actual CCI, not the enveloping situation. If you deploy for extended times, or work shifts as an LEO, your context will demand added training to cover for the additional demands on your system. For the context of this book, and combining De Becker et al and Bonnafaux's studies, we would like to be able to explode into action and sustain a fully anaerobic state, for somewhere between 5 seconds and about two minutes. The energy system that we need to prime then is our anaerobic glycolytic system. In terms of a pure CCI we need to at least be training for the following:

1. In relation to the ability to transition from non combative to completely combative,

    1.1. **Mobility should be such as to avoid range of motion related injuries.** This requires that you understand the mobility requirements of the specific actions to be taken. Mobility equates range of motion under load.

    1.2. **Breathing should be geared towards the anaerobic energy systems and not the aerobic energy system.** If you are caught off guard it means you will not have switched to the required breathing pattern. Trainees should be taught to exhale sharply, and through the mouth, two to three movements in, from here you can start forcing a breathing pattern that will help you remain anaerobic as well as not gassing out too fast.

2. In relation to the rest of the CCI,

    2.1. **We have found the best breathing pattern in this situation is strong in through the nose and a sharp exhale through the mouth.** Pure mouth breathing (in and out through the mouth) is a physiological effect signifying you have gassed out, but these effects can affect us backward as well, i.e. pure mouth breathing can signify to the brain there is an extra problem to be fixed, and you want to avoid this. This suggested breathing pattern will give you the best combination of performance versus anaerobic fuel management.

    2.2. **Anaerobic glycolysis is the primary energy pathway during a CCI.** Glycolysis is simply the breakdown of carbohydrates; the energy provided can last roughly between 10 seconds and 3 minutes. In the CCI context the duration that the glycolysis can last is strongly dependant on proper fitness and conditioning, breathing patterns, as well as injury. If at all possible, we want to end the CCI before this initial depletion, and as such we should focus our training predominantly within this timeframe but consistently towards faster and faster resolutions.

    2.3. **We have to train towards completion of the desired outcome.** The instructor needs to remove every option for the Trainee to stop mid CCI in Unscripted and Play environments. A mindset of finishing the encounter, and a will to fight until that resolution, is not automatically present in all individuals and should be nurtured at all times. When we provide training to clients, specifically when busy with Unscripted Training or Play Learning, we run a principle called Fix it Next Time. The three most frequent reasons we find Trainees stopping during a training repetition is:

2.3.1. Feeling like they did something wrong. Unless the mistake was of a critical nature, you should teach the trainee to Fix it Next Time. This mindset is predominantly present in Trainees coming from Technique heavy systems.

2.3.2. Getting tired or gassed. Rather than disengaging teach the Trainee to stabilize the CCI through Control, to do what they need to recover a breathing pattern that can allow them to carry on, and then to continue resolving the incident. In this case of energy depletion it can be that they started off without proper breathing (refer back to point 1.2. above), or never transitioned to a proper breathing pattern afterwards. If this was what happened then Fix it Next Time but let them continue resolving the current training repetition.

2.3.3. Getting stuck. Getting stuck should be treated the same way as above. The trainee needs to work until Control, take a moment to run an Assessment, and continue working for resolution. The only circumstances under which they should disengage and start again is if the Trainee made a critical error. Critical error meaning the error leads to immediate or imminent death.

THE MAUL

PART THREE — REQUIRED KNOWLEDGE BASE

THE MAUL

CHAPTER NINE – TARGETING AND MECHANISM OF INJURY

During any Close Combative Incident (CCI), but specifically during assaults, there is a need to quickly and accurately do what has to be done to stop the attack. This doesn't necessarily mean using lethal force; it can also mean disrupting the Opponent's ability to fight for long enough that they lose momentum or that the Trainee can escape, or possibly even creating the type of damage that causes the Opponent to lose their motivation to continue.

Making the decision of just how to do this in these dynamic encounters can be very tricky. It's one of the problems that new Trainees struggle with the most. The Combative Hierarchy of Needs (CHON) helps us to prioritize targeting, and to press our attacks or counter attacks in such a way that gives us the best odds of success. It is used in all CCI's as a mental model, as a way of plotting the Tactics required to achieve certain Goals. It is also used to plan Technique and Tactic selection and development. On the flip side of the coin, it also assists the Trainee in clearly understanding what needs to be protected, and purely so from the viewpoint of what will have the biggest influence on their ability to resolve the CCI. This is why it is called the Combative Hierarchy of Needs - it lists the physiological needs of the combatant in priority order.

Always remember: resolving a CCI does not necessarily imply killing. It may have to come to that, but it's not necessarily the specific outcome from the outset. As always context determines outcome. The self defense practitioner, LEO and soldier will have different outcomes pertaining to their context. The specific situation within the broader context should also influence outcome. For example, with the self defense practitioner, he is legally required to match his use of force with that of his Opponent. Read: He cannot shoot someone that is merely shoving him. The issue here is simply that we cannot pre-emptively decide what we are going to do in a situation that has not happened yet. We need to be able to Assess the unfolding scenario as it develops, and respond accordingly.

Next, it's important to understand that certain injuries, even having lethal potential, won't necessarily stop an attack and get you out of danger quickly. As example, and momentarily disregarding context or situation, consider the following very probably sequence of events. Suppose a Trainee was to stab an

Opponent in the chest three or four times during a CCI. These stabs will probably cause severe damage to the Opponent's chest cavity and lungs (let's not complicate it by including the heart, pericardial sac or large vessels surrounding the organs), the physiological effects of this severe damage might not manifest fast enough to stop the Opponent as quickly as the Trainee would like or needs to. Just how long it takes for this example's injury to manifest in such a way as to become useful in the CCI depends on a variety of factors. The simple truth is that this type of trauma to the chest cavity does not have the guaranteed physical effect of immediately stopping an attack from continuing. There is a strong likelihood that the Opponent will first experience a shortness of breath and possibly sense themselves gassing out. Interestingly enough the Opponent's brain will realize something is wrong and eventually send a limb to the injured area to feel it out via System 1. After doing so the Opponent might glance at the hand that checked the area, notice blood, and possibly start experiencing fluctuations in motivation. The problem for the Trainee is the duration of that process might cost them their life.

Part of the reason why the above process happens is because our brain prioritizes certain functions over others. It's something that is hardwired into all of us as a base survival instinct. For example, the function of balance has what might seem a disproportionally high priority placed on it by the brain. Our brain will divert almost all of its resources to fixing a balance related problem over anything else that might be happening in that moment, simply because balance, and proceeding movement capability, has such a high priority for us as a survival capability. If you remember as a child, rocking back on a chair and finding that tipping point unexpectedly where it felt like you were going to fall backward. That uncontrollable "freak out" moment is your brain fixing the balance problem as a priority over anything else. In that moment you are completely and totally unable to think of or do anything else.

It stands to reason then that knowing how the brain prioritizes these kinds of functions affords us an opportunity to exploit them in our Opponent as well as protect them for ourselves.

MECHANISM OF INJURY

Before we continue onto a more in-depth look at the CHON, it's important that we quickly establish exactly how edged and pointed weapons cause injury, or the "mechanism of injury". It may seem quite obvious to some and not so obvious to others, but either way it's worth noting.

There are really only two ways an edged and pointed weapon can injure severely enough that the results will eventually stop an attack. These are penetrating injuries from the point, and lacerations from the edge.

Penetrating injuries are considered by many to be the "more lethal" of the two simply because, in the vast majority of cases, it's what leads to a lethal outcome. While lacerations can be brutal and look extremely horrific they are quite survivable, even in cases where major blood vessels are severed, the human body is fairly robust and even has mechanisms for helping to slow or in some cases even stop blood loss from certain completely or neatly transacted blood vessels. In these cases the severed blood vessels go into vasospasm, retracting within the enveloping perivascular sheaths assisting with the staunching of blood flow.

Furthermore, lacerations can cause major bio-mechanical problems for the Opponent. Two methods in which it could do so are as follows: One, through severing skeletal muscle from the skeletal structure, and two, through either the transaction of or large and deep lacerations to and from the skeletal muscles. On the issues of cutting from the skeletal muscle simply imagine stripping off a large part of the forearm muscle (much or all of the digitorum superficialis / profundum and/or pollicis longus), the Opponent would severely struggle to hold onto their weapon.

Lastly, the graphic nature of lacerations may be enough to either cause psychogenic shock or to very seriously demotivate the Opponent.

All of these points are relevant to the Trainee's own situation. If we are badly cut, while it may look horrible, we need to realize that we are not out of the fight. While laceration injuries may be bad they are not the end. Penetrating injuries on the other hand we should consider as more serious. All of the major organs in the human body, as well as a few of the major arteries, require stabbing to be damaged. The heart, lungs and kidneys, as well as vessels like the aorta, subclavian artery, the jugular vein and the carotid artery, all are fairly deep within the body. Our bodies evolved to better protect the parts of us that are the most vital. In most instances you probably will not feel a stab wound until it begins to have a physiological effect on you. What we initially feel is the kinetic energy from the impact, as well as in most cases a burning sensation. Whether the Trainee realizes they feel it is not guaranteed. This is important to know and understand as it once again highlights the need to end the CCI as fast as possible.

This brings us neatly onto the concept of Timers and Switches.

TIMERS AND SWITCHES

The first category in the Combative Hierarchy of Needs falls into the class of a Timer. There are two types of Timer, a "Minutes" Timer and a "Seconds" Timer. Both of these Timers refer to injuries or disruptions which take time to have an effect. We first learned this concept of Timers (and Switches) from somewhere else, but we are not sure who first developed it. It would be great if anyone can assist us for we would gladly attribute it to them in future versions of the book.

That said, understanding that there is a delayed effect with Timers is the key. It means that even though the Trainee may have applied the kind of damage that could be lethal, it will only take effect later, as such, during this delay, the Trainee will need to either continue fighting or to avoid contact for the time it takes for the damage to have the desired effect. Just how long is variable. We need to understand that there are no explicit times which can be attributed to these types of injuries. There are many documented cases of people far outperforming or outliving the lethal expectations of the injury.

In 1942 W.E. Fairbairn published his book "Get Tough", which contained a chapter on Knife Combat. It also mentioned very hard and fast times for loss of consciousness and death from blood loss via major vessels. This book went on to become some of the most cited material for many others' work, and is even still quoted today when it comes to death by exsanguination. The problem is that the times quoted simply aren't true.

Extracted from "Get Tough" by W.E. Fairbairn:

ARTERY	LOSS OF CONSCIOUSNESS (Sec)	DEATH
Brachial	14	1 1/2 Min
Radial	30	2 Min
Carotid	5	12 Seconds
Subclavian	2	3 1/2 Seconds
Heart	Instantaneous Depending on Depth of Cut	3 Seconds
Stomach	Instantaneous Depending on Depth of Cut	

The times stated above are simply not realistic. With modern medical knowledge as well as firsthand accounts from combat medicine journals we know these times can vary wildly depend on the individual's own physiology and the nature of the injuries. More recently two papers were published by Darren Laur entitled "Unconsciousness and Death" in which Laur goes into this problem in much greater detail. The issue with most other previous research had been a total lack of any medical facts or professional opinion to back up the timings people were claiming for loss of consciousness and/or death by blood loss. In Laur's paper he cites two medical professionals, Dr Lorne David Porayko and Dr Christine Hall, who gave their professional insights into this subject. This we feel acts as a much more accurate guide to the unconsciousness and death via blood loss question.

First of all note that according to Dr Porayko we can assume the following:

• Loss of 750 ml to 1500 ml of blood would leave most average people "Dizzy".

• Loss of 1500 ml to 2 L of blood would leave most without the ability to stand upright.

This is quite a lot of blood. If you consider that the average 75 kg male has about 5 L of blood in their body, you can begin to understand how much blood volume needs to drop before the blood loss starts to realistically affect someone. Furthermore, these are generalized averages and there are variables which can influence these estimations. Since we cannot know the health and particular make up of the Opponent, we definitely cannot make assumptions about how fast they may or may not bleed out, lose consciousness and/or die. However, Dr Porayko and Dr Hall still give estimates for exsanguination for major blood vessels, let's consider them and note how different they are from the Fairburn schematic above:

BLOOD VESSEL	TIME
Carotid Artery	2 - 20 Minutes
Jugular Vein	15 - 60 Minutes
Sub Clavian Artery	2 - 20 Minutes
Sub Clavian Vein	15 - 60 Minutes
Brachial Artery	5 - 60 Minutes
Femoral Artery	5 - 60 Minutes
Aorta or Any Part of the Heart	1 - 2 Minutes

Both doctors based these estimates on current medical literature and their first hand experiences as trauma doctors. However, as already mentioned, we should be wary of internalizing and building on absolute rules when it comes to this issue. There are many accounts of people surviving injuries which simply should have killed them. The main outcome of this section is understanding the concept of a Timer; it is critical to know that there is a delayed effect to some of the damage the Trainee is causing and it is an important factor in the CCI.

In contrast with Timers, Switches are injuries and disruptions that have an immediate effect. There are honestly very few that fall into this category but we will touch them below.

When considering the Timers and the Switches from the point of view of the Trainee, meaning the Opponent has affected a Timer or a Switch on the Trainee, the following needs to be noted. A Switch will technically not be noticed by the Trainee. The Timer might be noticed. If the Timer is noticed it should be treated as a countdown Timer, as in, the Trainee should very clearly understand that there is now a rapidly closing window of opportunity in which the CCI can be resolved to their benefit. At times, the brain will struggle to make this connection, especially if the type of injury is not known to the brain. The art lies in *telling* the brain what has happened, and *deciding* on a course of action. This is an extremely difficult skill to master in the absence of experience or extremely accurate training as System 1's autopilot might need to be suppressed by System 2's more willful functioning. Thought should always be put into how to train this.

We will attach the CHoN schematic below, but first let's have a concise look at its elements:

1. **TIMERS - MINUTES**

    1.1. The first Timer covers injuries and disruptions where the delay on the effect spans minutes.

    1.2. Described as injuries and disruptions with a high priority which eventually impair function. If left untreated, some injuries will eventually lead to death. This type of Timer would attempt to affect the following:

        1.2.1   Adequate blood volume

        1.2.2   Respiratory system integrity

1.2.3   Adequate respiration

1.2.4   Perfusion

1.3 Any use of force which causes injury or disruption to the above systems will take the longest time to have a physiological effect, and as such, the longest time to create an opportunity to stop the attack. This means that, for example, if the Trainee managed to get a few good stabs into your Opponent's lungs, it may not be enough to immediately end the attack. There's a very high probability the Opponent wouldn't even feel or register the injuries inflicted until after his body begins to weaken and slow down from inadequate respiration and subsequently lack of perfusion.

2. <u>TIMERS - SECONDS</u>

2.1 This Timer covers injuries and disruptions where the delay on the effect spans seconds.

2.2 Described as injuries and disruptions with a higher priority and that quickly restrict function. If left untreated, some injuries will quickly lead to death. Concerning the non lethal items on this list, it is important to understand that they are a very high priority to the brain as they effect specific secondary needs required to sustain survival capability. System 1 will divert a lot of resources to fixing or dealing with these problems.

2.2.1   Open airway

2.2.2   Unimpaired respiration

2.2.3   Functioning CNS

2.2.4   Balance

2.2.5   Structure

2.2.6   Sight

2.3 When it comes to balance, structure and sight, these are disruptions which are unlikely to cause any direct critical injury to the attacker, but will divert the brain's resources away from thinking about the fight to fixing the problem. As such, disrupting balance and structure is going to cause a momentary lapse in your Opponent's ability to fight you. This is something you can directly affect or could happen as a result of the environment. If for whatever reason your attacker slips, trips or starts to fall, it can be used as an opportunity. Likewise covering or hurting an Opponent's eyes will cause System 1 to try and fix the issue of sight and subsequently you will be provided with another window of opportunity.

3. SWITCHES - INSTANT

3.1. Switches are injuries or disruptions which have an immediate effect.

3.2. Described as injuries and disruptions with the highest priority and that immediately removes function. Leads to death or paralysis. There are really only two ways to affect a switch on the Opponent:

3.2.1. Severe or critical damage to the CNS

3.2.2. Cardiac arrest

3.3 Forcing either of these outcomes may be a necessity in certain contexts, or become a necessity as a CCI unfolds. Please find the CHON Schematic below:

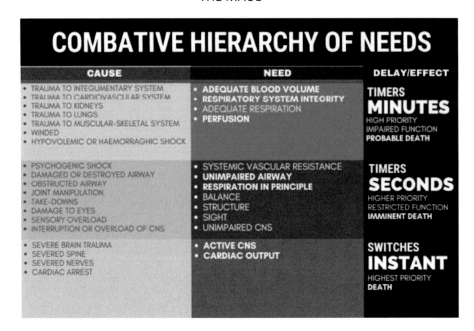

COMBATIVE HIERARCHY OF NEEDS

CAUSE	NEED	DELAY/EFFECT
• TRAUMA TO INTEGUMENTARY SYSTEM • TRAUMA TO CARDIOVASCULAR SYSTEM • TRAUMA TO KIDNEYS • TRAUMA TO LUNGS • TRAUMA TO MUSCULAR-SKELETAL SYSTEM • WINDED • HYPOVOLEMIC OR HAEMORRAGHIC SHOCK	• ADEQUATE BLOOD VOLUME • RESPIRATORY SYSTEM INTEGRITY • ADEQUATE RESPIRATION • PERFUSION	**TIMERS** **MINUTES** HIGH PRIORITY IMPAIRED FUNCTION **PROBABLE DEATH**
• PSYCHOGENIC SHOCK • DAMAGED OR DESTROYED AIRWAY • OBSTRUCTED AIRWAY • JOINT MANIPULATION • TAKE-DOWNS • DAMAGE TO EYES • SENSORY OVERLOAD • INTERRUPTION OR OVERLOAD OF CNS	• SYSTEMIC VASCULAR RESISTANCE • UNIMPAIRED AIRWAY • RESPIRATION IN PRINCIPLE • BALANCE • STRUCTURE • SIGHT • UNIMPAIRED CNS	**TIMERS** **SECONDS** HIGHER PRIORITY RESTRICTED FUNCTION **IMMINENT DEATH**
• SEVERE BRAIN TRAUMA • SEVERED SPINE • SEVERED NERVES • CARDIAC ARREST	• ACTIVE CNS • CARDIAC OUTPUT	**SWITCHES** **INSTANT** HIGHEST PRIORITY **DEATH**

TARGETING

When considering how to affect a specific Switch or Timer, always remember that there are many complications that can arise from becoming too fixated on reaching a specific target. You may tell yourself that "I'm going to stab for the heart" but practically whether that transpires can be drastically different from expectation. This is the essential importance in understanding the CHON. It doesn't require you to have a preplanned sequence of Techniques to achieve an outcome. If you know the outcome you want, and you know which targets will get you there, you can choose the best route that is presented to you in the moment instead of trying to force one that may not be there.

It is also within this reality, that targets don't always present themselves as desired or expected, that pre-planned sequences or combinations can fail. Consider the following:

1. An Opponent flinching and collapsing into the Trainee unexpectedly in reaction to the Trainee's opening move. Should this happen, the Opponent may well be much closer than which the Trainee's brain originally planned for, i.e. the second and third movement of the combination may not be relevant anymore.

2. Another consideration would be an Opponent wearing really baggy or heavy clothing. In this case the clothing might be obscuring body composition and/or actual targets; that makes targeting a specific place on their body extremely difficult.

3. Lastly, for whatever reason, you simply miss and you don't have a backup sequence or "extra" move in the combination.

These are just three examples that show some of the difficulties in having elaborate pre-planned movement sequences and/or combinations. Knowing where Switches and Timers are situated on our Opponents means we always have access to something. The only thing left to do is to ensure that we have trained in such a way that we are able to adapt to targets as and when they present themselves.

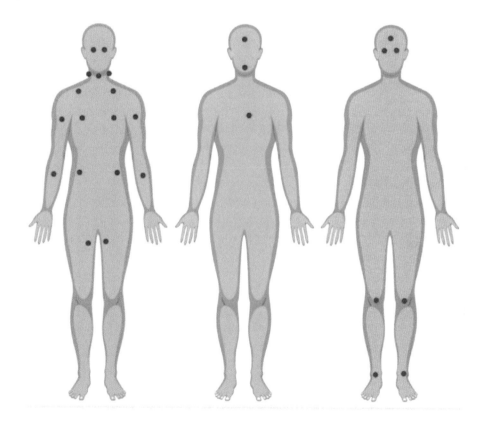

The above diagram highlights specific areas where Timers, Switches, and as an addition, Base targets can be found.

1. THE ORANGE BODY

These are both Minute & Second Timers and include the following:

1.1. **Eyes.** Targeting the eyes will at the very least cause a flinch reaction which the Trainee can capitalize on. If the eyes are covered, or damage is inflicted to the eyes, it's unlikely to be fatal but can very likely become a fight ender or buy the Trainee a window of opportunity for either escape or pressing forward towards the next goal.

1.2. **Throat/neck.** There is a reason why The Maul's motto is "Always go for the throat". It is a target that affords us a lot of potential condensed into one area. Any disruption to the airway (windpipe) will cause a momentary lapse in focus, even if the injury is unlikely to be fatal it buys time and provides the Trainee with options. The neck also contains two major blood vessels in the Carotid Artery and Jugular Vein, opening these will cause serious blood loss. This area is exposed and not naturally well defended in the way that our hearts and brains are shielded by bone. A good pikal stab and rip through the side of the neck can and likely will do serious damage to both the airway and blood vessels. Alternatively, when no edged or pointed weapon is available, the area also contains four large nerve complexes that are very susceptible to blunt force.

1.3. **Sub-clavian artery.** This is a major artery situated slightly below and behind the clavicle towards the first rib. It's actually fairly well protected but can be accessed by going straight down behind the clavicle.

1.4. **Lung/chest cavity.** Interfering with the integrity of either/both of the lungs or chest cavity will lead to various complications, all of which will need medical intervention. Note that most injuries purely to these two targets will take time to have an effect.

1.5. **Brachial & radial arteries.** Located in the upper and lower arm respectively, and because of the propensity for the flailing of the arms to start if your attacker shifts into System 1, these major arteries might be more presented than others and as such offer good targets.

1.6. **Kidneys.** While severe damage to the kidney itself will not be an immediate or imminent attack stopper, it is an extremely sensitive target and the associated pain might very well disrupt your Opponent's performance. As a target area they are very exposed albeit the Trainee first needs to get rear access to the Opponent.

1.7. **Femoral artery.** A major blood vessel located in the upper inner thigh. Can cause major blood loss but can also be quite difficult to reach.

2. THE BLUE BODY

These are all Switches.

> **2.1. Central Nervous System (CNS).** The CNS in lay terms refers to the spinal cord and the brain. Causing massive trauma to the brain, or disrupting or severing the communication between the spinal cord and the brain will cause a relatively instant shut down, which is why we call it a Switch. Damaging the CNS with bare hands or certain types of smaller cold weapons, say for instance an EDC folder, is not easy. In this case it would probably be more sensible to aim damage to the occipital protuberance or alternatively the c-spine area, that is, the first couple of vertebrae where the neck joins the skull. It's possible to get a blade between the vertebrae and sever the spinal cord, but it's not necessarily an easy or clean cut task.

> **2.2 Heart.** Massive trauma to the heart will cause a Switch effect due to a massive loss of blood pressure. Getting to the heart in a CCI context and when a clear shot with a firearm is not possible, as is the case with the CNS, is not an easy thing. It is naturally well protected behind skeletal structures and an Opponent will also instinctively protect the area. To complicate it further knowing how to accurately pin point the organ on someone who is moving, presumably clothed, and also trying to fight you, will further compound the problem.

3. THE GREY BODY

This represents what we call Base Targets. These are targets that will disrupt the balance of the Opponent either through damaging the base or, conversely, moving the centre of gravity over the base.

> 3.1. **Knees, ankles & feet**. Stabilizing joints like the knee are vulnerable to kicks, both from behind when the Opponent's weight is on the leg, or from the side to injure or destabilize the joint itself. Damaging either/or the ligaments and tendons around the knees and/or ankles will severely influence movement and balance. Alternatively, immobilizing the feet while forcing movement of the body will cause the Opponent's centre of gravity to travel over their base.

> 3.2. **Head.** Where the head goes the body usually follows. Being able to manipulate your opponents head is a quick way to unbalance and compromise his structure.

> 3.3. **Eyes.** Humans very naturally and instinctively pull away from anything that interferes with their vision. Forcing a hand into the Opponent's immediate field of vision can have the double effect of a Timer as well

as initiating a break of structure which can in turn be transitioned into a Takedown.

Having a good understanding of targeting allows System 1 do what it does best: To select targets at high speed within a dynamic environment, as and when they become available, to achieve the desired outcome. The ultimate goal is to dynamically but accurately target within the ever changing CCI. This ability allows us to adapt and change according to what is unfolding in CCI, without compromising on what we want to ultimately achieve.

CHAPTER TEN: ARM YOURSELF

The ARM Yourself model was originally developed as an answer to the question: "So exactly when do I hit him?" This question came from a female client that was struggling to pinpoint the exact moment in which to take action, or rather, to Move. The reality though is that many Trainees struggle with this question. Whether Moving relates to running away, screaming, striking, stabbing or squeezing a trigger, there are always better or worse moments in which to do so. For us, the challenge was that the models that were available for this decision making process lacked two things: One, they were often lengthy and complicated. We needed something easy to remember and even easier to deploy. And two, we could find little evidence of any actual recent brain research in their knowledge base. Which begged the question: How do we really know how well they work? Through science, experience, or just anecdotal? ARM Yourself is one compilation of our research that provides a method of dealing with the essential problem of when to act. When properly applied ARM Yourself is a powerful mental discipline that will significantly increase the Trainee's reaction time.

The name ARM Yourself is an acronym which stands for "Assess, Ready, Move". They are three phases or stages and are to be accomplished from the left to the right. Note that this process is different than the CCI Resolution Process (Process) featured later in the book. The CCI Process was developed for use within the actual CCI. ARM Yourself is the launch pad for any Move option - whether it be engaging in a CCI or not. Also note that ARM Yourself is a completely developed stand alone model. In this The Maul we have provided only a brief discussion of the model's main components, a complete discussion unfortunately doesn't fall into the scope of this book.

ARM Yourself is the process of identifying specific indicators or determinants, mentally priming the brain for action, and taking the action once the priming qualifiers are met. The actual performance enhancement is locked into the step of priming. What are we priming? We are priming System 1 using System 2. We are not getting in System 1's way, we are just predetermining, or suggesting, when and how System 1 should take over. This act of priming offers two immense benefits:

1. We negate any possible freeze effect due to sudden and unexpected stimulus.

2. We have offered System 1 a sensibly selected option, thus capitalizing on System 1's speed but minimizing its ability to select a wrong or hazardous Move option.

With this foundation laid, let's move forward to a concise explanation of each phase.

ASSESS

If you are practicing good Situational Awareness it means you have developed the discipline of continuously Assessing. What are we Assessing? Primarily two groups of variables: Pre Incident iNdicators (PINs) and Tactic Determinants (TDs). As mentioned earlier, a thorough discussion on these groups are beyond the scope of this book, but we do encourage everyone to learn more about them. In terms of PINs, groundbreaking work has been done by Patrick Van Horn and captured in his book *Left of Bang*, as well as by Gavin De Becker and specifically in his books *Just 2 Seconds* and *The Gift of Fear*. These are great places to start for anyone wanting to delve into this topic.

That said, Van Horn builds his work around a linear schematic containing a basic timeline with an incident marker (see below), the incident being "bang". Everything happening before the incident is left of bang, and everything happening post incident is right of bang.

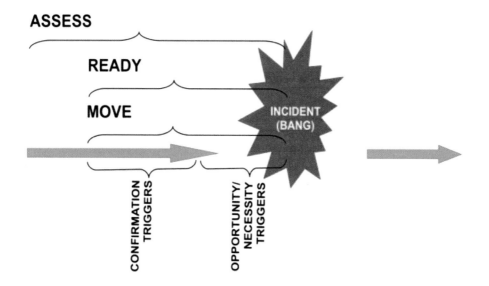

The Assess phase is predominantly left of bang, that is, pre-incident, but it can run into the incident as well. Whether it does or does not relates to whether we have retained or lost initiative, i.e. whether we saw the attack coming or whether we were caught off guard.

We know that critical incidents are extremely dynamic. They continuously develop and events keep unfolding until the incident has been resolved. Thus, we need to develop the discipline of continuously hunting for these developments - these dynamic changes. However, if our training does not include active and continuous assessment, we will never develop this discipline. This means that any training for CCIs need to include Assessment components. Assessing is a function of the brain and it needs to be trained and developed as such.

Examples of changes could be something as simple as a committed attacker suddenly backing off and wanting to disengage (internal changes in the Opponent) or as complicated as an unarmed encounter suddenly becoming an armed encounter. If we are not training to Assess then we will miss the developments that can dictate our best course of action.

READY

The Ready phase acts as a Trigger setting discipline in which we prime our brains for the actions of the Movement phase. *It is the mental process of GETTING READY to Move.*

Setting a Trigger is like drawing an imaginary line in the sand. Mentally we are telling ourselves that if our Opponent steps over that line then we will act. IF the Opponent steps over that line THEN we will *squeeze* the Trigger. Trigger setting then is the weaponization of a fundamental IF THIS THEN THAT brain algorithm. This algorithm is already foundational to the brain's functioning and execution. We are simply using it for our purposes.

A Trigger is a pre-determined qualifier, set mentally, and that will launch a chosen action once met. Knowledge of and tactics on selecting Trigger qualifiers, as well as the act of Trigger setting, should both be incorporated into all training sessions. Training methodologies should be developed in such a way that Trainees are forced to set Triggers in most repetitions.

We have broken Triggers into three main groups:

CONFIRMATION TRIGGERS:

These are Triggers which are set before the critical incident has occurred. A potential but as yet unconfirmed actual threat has been identified. I have initiative. We continue to Assess. The qualifiers are observations that confirm the potential threat as an actual threat. The Trigger is squeezed immediately upon confirmation of the threat.

Examples may be:

- There is some form of commotion, including what sounds like terrified screams, outside my classroom. IF I hear gunfire outside my class room at school THEN I will immediately barricade the door.
- I have chased down a suspect of a homicide, he is verbally combative and doesn't want to remove his right hand from his pocket. It doesn't appear to be a firearm as there is no print. He is not submitting to my commands. IF this guy draws a weapon from that pocket THEN I'm shooting.

Priming yourself in this way reduces the amount of time and potential hesitation involved in making the decision in the moment.

OPPORTUNITY TRIGGERS:

These are Triggers which are set during the critical incident. There is an actual threat but the threat is not yet causing me harm. I have lost initiative. Because I have lost initiative I might risk injury if Moving at the wrong time or in the wrong way. We continue to Assess. The qualifiers are observations that confirm what has been selected as a good enough to perfect window of opportunity to Move. The Trigger is squeezed the moment that the window presents itself.

If you observe the schematic above you will notice that Opportunity Triggers run in a very small space before the incident is started, as well as into the incident.

Examples may be:

- Three robbers run into my house, two are armed with crowbars and one with a firearm, they have caught me unawares. I carry a firearm. The Opponent's firearm is already pointing at me and I cannot outdraw his trigger squeeze. IF the firearm robber significantly lowers his firearm or leaves the room THEN I will draw my firearm. (Obviously this assumes you are able to access your firearm fast enough and whilst under duress.)
- A knife wielding robber has stopped me and is demanding money. He is standing very close to me and hyper focused on me. I have firm reason to believe that giving him my wallet is not going to ensure not being stabbed. IF he looks away THEN I am going to shove him hard and run away.

Opportunities can be coincidental or manufactured, we talk about waiting and working for opportunity. But, if we don't prime ourselves for them whilst remaining in a constant state of Assessment, then there is a good chance we will either be too slow or miss them completely when they arise.

NECESSITY TRIGGERS:

These Triggers are set during the critical incident. There is an actual threat and there is an immediate and urgent need for action, irrespective of the consequences. The actions associated with these triggers are less pre-planned and more based on making the best of a bad situation. A Necessity Trigger means that you are about to be seriously injured or killed by someone or something, and you need to Move because if you don't, you *will* suffer severe damage or die. In these cases the odds are that doing something is better than doing nothing.

MOVE – TAKING ACTION				
MOVE OPTION	SUBVERT	ESCAPE	DEFEND	MITIGATE
WHEN TO CONSIDER	Possible or Confirmed Threat	Confirmed Threat	Confirmed Threat	Threat Passed
DANGER LEVEL	Not in danger	In danger	In danger	Not in danger
TRIGGERS APPLICABLE	Confirmation Trigger	Opportunity / Necessity Trigger	Opportunity / Necessity Trigger	
CONCISE DEFINTION	Anything that can be done to prevent the threat from launching an attack	Anything that can be done to escape the threat and danger	Anything that can be done to stop the attack	Anything that can be done to mitigate the fallout of the attack

Examples may be:

- A knife wielding robber has started to assault me and I have been stabbed multiple times. IF I get the opportunity to disengage THEN I will do so and run away. During the CCI I manage to trip the robber, he loses his balance and starts to fall. I disengage and run.
- An active shooter is in the final moments of breaking through the barricade. IF he breaks through THEN I will rush him and fight him for his weapon.

The main difference between Opportunity Triggers and Necessity Triggers lies in determining when it's BEST to Move and when it's ESSENTIAL to Move.

MOVE

As with the Assess and Ready phases above, a full treatment on Move options is beyond the scope of this specific book. We have however attached our Move Model, it provides the framework through which we would select Move options for specific phases of critical incidents and CCIs. Please note that the DEFEND option essentially denotes any combative action taken, whether offensive or defensive in purpose.

PART FOUR – SYSTEMATIZING THE SOLUTION: THE MAUL

THE MAUL

CHAPTER ELEVEN: THE MAUL

WHAT IS THE MAUL?

The Maul is essentially an edged and pointed weapon based close combat system. It is robust and versatile enough that it can be used within any context and whether defensively or offensively. Rather than relying on purely endemic tactics (not that some of them aren't effective for certain outcomes) and hearsay, the goal was to develop an approach guided and directed by actual cutting edge brain research.

The name "The Maul" refers back to the animal kingdom. The Mirriam-Webster dictionary defines it as follows: to mangle, to injure with deep disfiguring wounds by cutting, tearing, or crushing. Animals maul. They also go for the throat. When they need to kill it is very natural for them to direct their chaotic movement towards the throat area as they know injury there can be critical. We have adopted these two strategies into The Maul. We constantly work towards inflicting massive damage on our Opponent, but with the throat being the primary target of interest. As you will see in our Development Principles below we deploy these tactics only when legally justified to do so. Again, remember, that the book has now rounded the corner away from the knowledge base applied to CCIs, and towards the knowledge base applied specifically to edge and point use.

Before we continue, note this final observation: Animals maul in what frequently appears to be complete chaos. However, it is only the movement that is chaotic, they actually have very definite intention with two very clear outcomes in mind: To dominate or to kill. Thus, we have adopted the term Directed Chaos into The Maul. The Maul then is an attempt to master the chaos of System 1, in such a way that we can achieve our outcome of stopping an attack, through either domination or critical injury.

DEVELOPMENT PRINCIPLES OF THE MAUL

In refining The Maul we set ourselves six development principles. These are not The Ten Principles of the Maul. These principles come into play when considering the addition or change of any Techniques, Tactic or Procedure in the system.

1. **Tactics should be morally and legally justifiable**. There is a lot of really good material available on the legalities of self defense as well as on the use of force. We aren't going to delve too deeply into this topic, other than to say the following: Both the authors of this book strongly believe that all human life intrinsically has value and should only be damaged or taken when justified and needed. Both authors also firmly believe in the rule of law, and as far as it remains up to us, we will always train and develop tactics that function well within the rule of law, specifically when that is the context of the Trainee. Where it is not the context of the Trainee we adjust training accordingly. Do not confuse this with a lack of efficacy in our Tactics, or a lack of will in our motivation. If you feel otherwise, that is your privilege.

2. **Techniques, Tactics or Procedures should function well in System 1**. We have discussed this point in the chapter Implications on Training Methodology.

3. **Techniques, Tactics and Procedures should be developed to strongly demotivate and/or quickly incapacitate**. This point aligns with our desire to end the attack as fast as possible and flows from our adoption of the concept of a maul. In terms of demotivation we favor techniques and tactics that will affect big gashing wounds, in terms of incapacitation we favor techniques that will influence the CNS or blood pressure the fastest; the neck and throat area being our primary target of interest.

4. **Complicated, contrary or single use movement patterns should be avoided**. Any movement that doesn't fit or feel comfortable with the bulk of the existing movement patterns should be avoided as it creates unnecessary load on training times. The Technique set should be compact and flow well together.

5. **The Maul should function well within other existing systems**. It should be clear by now that The Maul is primarily concerned with edge and point performance in System 1. There are many other effective close combat and martial arts system available. Although The Maul is able to, we are not proposing in any way that The Maul should replace these. Instead, The Maul should be an added toolset and we should be able to transition to it when needed regardless of other training.

6. **Always focus on gross movement patterns**. Essentially our opponent's body can only go in one of five directions: Left, right, forward, backwards and

down. His arm can essentially only come forward, or go backwards; predominantly the arm will move from the inside to the outside, outside to the inside, top to bottom or bottom to top, albeit at a myriad of angles. Tactics should predominantly follow the rough process of adapting to these very few gross movement patterns. Technique selection, as well as their deployment during a CCI, should be modeled on these movement patterns as well. In terms of Technique deployment, one of the essential requirements for this to be effective are the disciplines of longer contact, positive pressure and Continuous Assessment. We want to feel where the Opponent is moving to. We will obviously develop these thoughts as we go, but seeing as this specific item may come across as quite abstract, here is an example: Instead of teaching a Trainee a specific takedown as a response to an Opponent's specific Technique, we will teach them to feel for a change in the gross movement pattern and to select a Technique based on that change. Although this approach assumes that we have trained at least one useable takedown through System 2, it ensures a couple of things:

6.1. The trainee is Continuously Assessing during the CCI through tactile feedback - making his response selection faster.

6.2. We can shorten the amount of Techniques we teach him as one or two good robust Techniques should more than account for slight variations in a gross movement pattern. Again, this amounts to a speed increase as we've decreased the options his brain has to consider before selecting a response.

6.3. System 1 can become masterful at deploying one or two good robust Techniques due to volume of training in constantly changing Unscripted Training and Play Learning environments.

PRIMARY TACTIC DETERMINANTS FOR THE MAUL

Edged and pointed CCIs have three main Tactic Determinants that we need to strongly consider. These three dynamics are highly prevalent in all edged and pointed CCIs and, as such, The Maul has attempted to firmly address them as a system.

1. **Edged and pointed weapons have specific range requirements**. This range both determines what distance an attack can be launched from as

well as sustained from. We work with a concept called *an Arm and a Step*. The *Arm and a Step* belonging to that of the opponent. Thus we spend a lot of time working with our clients on assessing and adapting to dynamic range changes. Also note this is the primary reason why you very seldom see the weapon before the attack; if the attacker deployed the weapon too far in advance the other party can simply leave or possibly deploy a firearm. In The Maul then, we maintain an *Arm and a Step* for as long as possible. If we have an opportunity or there is a movement constraint of some sort we might close the distance specifically to one that allows for Control of the weapon arm.

2. **Compact angles of attack are deployed in fast and repetitive movements**. Referring back to our stab drill explained in the chapter a Short Note on Time Frames, when assaulting with a knife we can consistently generate between 7 - 11 stabs in around 2 seconds. The reason for this was explained in the previous chapter. When we deploy small and tight arcs and short patterns of movement it means our brains are able to adapt and change these arcs and patterns quicker and with more frequency. In doing so the attacker can work his or her way around the defenses of the victim. In The Maul then we purposefully deploy this tactic offensively. We have also created or adopted and streamlined certain defensive movement patterns that specifically work better against these movement patterns.

3. **Most attacks are led with the empty hand**. It is very infrequent that edge and point weapon users lead with huge sweeping arcs of the blade. It is the most natural movement in the world to try and control or defend with the empty hand. In relation to control the user will frequently try and grab a limb, hair, or piece of clothing, as a method of securing the victim for the attack. More advanced users will also control in such a manner that they get access to the outside or rear (dead side) of the target. Conversely if defending, the empty hand will be used a shield for the rest of the body. In The Maul we use this empty hand ourselves, more on this later though. We've also incorporated specific drills for dealing with the Opponent's empty hand.

THE TEN PRINCIPLES OF THE MAUL

1. **ALWAYS manage balance. We do so through the following strategies:**

   1.1. Take smaller steps and allow your brain to shuffle your feet along with you. This will ensure that your base always stays under your centre of gravity.

   1.2. Do not reach or over extend to reach a target. Learn to pick appropriate targets, to range effectively, and to either let your target come to you or let your feet take you to your target.

   1.3. If the space between you and the Opponent has closed don't hesitate to use them as a base or post to manage your own balance. With a post we mean that you either lean or hang on them in such a way that they become a part of your base.

   1.4. If balance has been compromised either fall in such a way as to disengage and set up a next move, or take your Opponent with you in such a way that you create pain, or damage him, during the takedown.

1. **Trust the weapon**. Most individuals that haven't used an edge or pointed weapon combatively have a disconnect concerning the damage it causes and the ease in which it can do so when used effectively. This leads to an overemphasis on unnecessary details in the weapon's use. Trainees should be steered away from this and simply trust the weapon to do what it should.

2. **Weapon interchangeability**. The movement patterns selected for The Maul allows for the widest range of weapon interchangeability. This is why we use pikal style (tip down, edge back, possible curved backwards) blades. All the movement patterns that work with the pikal style blade will work with a tip up blade. All the movement patterns that work with a tip up blade won't work with pikal style. Movement patterns that work with the pikal style blade also work with most pointed and many improvised weapons (pens, tv remote, fork, screwdriver etc). Lastly, most of The Maul's primary movement patterns also function well when unarmed as the pikal style blade and grip can be exchanged for either a striking hammer fist or a grabbing hand.

3. **Drive Forward and Outside**. Whether the decision was made to close range, or whether the closing is forced by the opponent, drive forward and stay as

close to the attacking limb as possible. If able, navigate towards the outside of that limb as this is tactically the safest position to be in. In all of this movement maintain positive pressure on the opponent and especially on the attacking limb as this will provide the fastest feedback for adaptation.

4. **Live in the box**. Hips to shoulders, left to right. This is the working space. Whether defending or attacking, all of the attention should be focused here. If a height or level change is required use the legs, do not let the arms go out of the box. Apart from the fact that this will increase your protection of the vitals it adds two other immense benefits: When properly trained to work in this space you will naturally develop tight arcs and shorter patterns of movement, this will lead to a definite increase in quickness. Also, in terms of power generation and dexterity, both their sweet spots lie within the box. Dexterity closer to the chest and power extended forward from the chest.

5. **No hyperextension**. Under no circumstances should an arm be extended fully, whether forward, to the sides, across the chest, down or up. There should always be a slight bend at the elbow (around 135º). This will ensure shorter, but also much more controlled, movement patterns. Also, and assuming we cannot escape an edged and pointed CCI and HAVE to engage at close range, it is important to remember that the basis of any defense against such an attack is Control of the weapon wielding arm. If the arm holding the knife can't move the knife can't move. This works both ways though, when your arm is hyper extended its long and less quick meaning your opponent can more easily grab or pin it.

6. **Stay behind a limb**. Always keep the torso behind either the weapon or the empty hand. This requires that the elbow moves to the torso's centre line before deploying any Technique. This movement of the elbow might require transverse motion (twisting) in the torso.

7. **Continuous piston action**. Keep both arms in play at all times. Ingraining a piston type action in the Flow Drill will increase the odds of this happening. The left and right arm should alternate forward in a controlled rhythmic pattern during the Flow Drill. It's important for the instructor to monitor this dynamic as it displays whether the Trainee is in a dueling or The Maul mindset. In a dueling mindset the Trainee will start to spar with his opponent picking stabs one by one. With The Maul we want to go at the opponent full speed and aggressively, trusting System 1 to deploy

movements and create damage that will strongly demotivate and/or quickly incapacitate.

8. **One limb at a time.** Apart from any instance where a decision is made to apply both hands to the Opponent, the Trainee should be in the habit of having only one limb extended at a time. If the Trainee is driving the piston action successfully this shouldn't be a problem. This is primarily a risk management issue. At the speeds and dynamism of a full blown CCI there is always risk to damage oneself with the weapon. The possibility of cutting off your own finger is real.

9. **ALWAYS. GO. FOR. THE. THROAT.** By Go for the Throat we mean any neck target. It can be to the side of the neck nerve complexes or large vessels, it can be to the actual throat or oesophagus, or it can be to the c-spine or the occipital protuberance at the back. Learn to work for and direct the chaos towards the neck area. The neck area is also very susceptible to unarmed force making it a good target for an opening move, as part of a combination, or as target for a dedicated entry.

PROGRESS DIFFERENCES FROM OTHER SYSTEMS

THE BAD

1. **Experience of chaos**. Training in The Maul is a very chaotic initial experience. Our experience is that those versed in violence, those that come from an operational background, those that come from a grappling art, or those that come without any frame of reference, adapt easier to the initial phase. Those that come from Krav Maga, traditional martial arts, certain RBSD, or any other highly systematised and controlled training environment, struggle immensely with both the physical and emotional experience of this chaos.

2. **Less immediate gratification**. In commercial and controlled training environments the Trainee is set up for success. A Technique or Procedure is trained within a highly scripted scenario and it is practiced for high quantity of repetitions. This means by the end of the session the Trainee can successfully apply that movement pattern within that script. This leads to a strong sense of gratification and an experience success. The Maul in its initial phases does not offer this. It offers failure

and a reality check.

3. **More injuries**. The Maul recommends training with pikal style blunt metal blades. Baring taking care around the eyes (including wearing protection) the whole body is an open target. Contact is always made and the knives scratch, lacerate and bruise. Takedowns are part of our Tactics and the falling bruises as well. This teaches both respect for the weapon and will to fight.

THE GOOD

1. **Humility.** The reality check from experiencing the chaos of an edged and pointed weapon CCI leads to an honest humility. This humility is good as it fosters a teachable spirit and attitude. The Maul, ultimately, is an environment and approach where consistent self exploration and organic learning is nurtured and encouraged. The Trainee's ego however has to be in check or it will hamper their experience in this regard.

2. **The Six Week Milestone**. Even though we call it the Six Week Milestone it's not really a cleanly defined span of time. What we find though, is that around the six week marker, a Trainee makes a significant advancement in their ability. We suspect it relates to the time needed to program System 1 in the Flow and Chaos Drills. After this marker gets hit training becomes a much different experience. As the core movement patterns are now ingrained the brain has more capacity for creativity, problem solving and the development of personal style (which we highly encourage).

3. **Fast progression**. After the Six Week Milestone is hit progression becomes much faster as it is now driven by System 1's conditioning within the Unscripted Training and Play Learning environments. Essentially what we have done with The Maul is to develop a very Technique lean but Goal driven system. Instead of keeping the Trainee busy for years and years with ever expanding lists of Techniques, we have selected the fewest amounts of robust and effective Techniques that we could get away with, and developed a training methodology that allows for much faster mastery of Correct Execution.

CHAPTER TWELVE: PROCESS

THE CCI RESOLUTION PROCESS SCHEMATIC (THE MAUL PROCESS)

Please note that the resolution process we use in CCIs and The Maul is linear with cyclical components in between every Goal. In an ideal world we will resolve the CCI in one pass and from the left to right. More on this in the CCI Process Principles below:

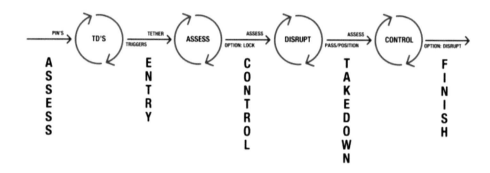

THE MAUL PROCESS

ASSESS

1. **GOAL DEFINITION**: Identifying of PINs, TDs and Trigger Setting. Basically the Assess and Ready phases of ARM Yourself.

2. **GOAL INSIGHT**: Explained in the ARM Yourself chapter.

3. **PRO TIPS**:

3.1. Let range guide your assessments. If someone is in medium approaching close range focus your assessments on Threat Indicators (weapons, hands, positioning, dominant or uncomfortable behavior clusters) and TDs rather than situational PINs.

3.2. Amateurs assess whether they can handle a situation, professionals assess how they will handle a situation. Trigger setting shouldn't just be based on the situation, they should also contain options based on TDs. Scan for available targets, compromises in your Opponents defenses, possible balance and structure exploitations.

3.3. Adjust your stance and weight in preparation. Remember that we Live in the Box. Arms should be up and in front of the torso as in an interview stance. Feet should be staggered comfortably into a stance that can both absorb incoming force as well as launch an entry. When you explode into the Entry your movement will start in your rear leg. Shift your weight accordingly without it being apparent.

4. **WHEN TO TRANSITION**: Transitioning is dependent on the Trigger that you have set. For a Confirmation Trigger you would transition the moment that the threat is confirmed. For an Opportunity Trigger the moment that an apt opportunity presents itself. If you were caught unawares the Necessity Triggers kicks in and automatically skip to Entry or Control.

ENTRY

1. **GOAL DEFINITION**: A Technique used to close range.

2. **GOAL INSIGHT**:

2.1. The gross movement pattern of the Technique should ideally work offensively as well as defensively.

2.2. Offensive capability. The Entry Technique in itself should be highly effective as a way of delivering force; the Entry Technique should ideally be an impact strike able to reach and deliver enough force to knock the Opponent out or down in one movement.

2.3. Defensive capability. Should the Trainee be caught unawares, the

Entry Technique should be robust and quickly deployable by System 1.

2.4. Robustness. The Technique should cover as wide a range of incoming attacks and permutations as possible. This means that a single Entry Technique should be able to handle many different angles and ranges of attacks.

3. **PRO TIPS**:

3.1. Be wary of systems that teach multiple Entry Techniques. The one author of this book trained and qualified as instructor in multiple Krav Maga systems. One of those systems offers 11 options per side to deal with an incoming straight punch. Another system offers at least five entries per side to deal with various incoming attacks. This is highly inefficient and frequently because of two reasons: First, lack of depth of understanding and developmental thought in the system, and two, an issue in commercial systems that need high volumes of content to retain students over long periods of time.

3.2. Train your Entry like you would any other strike: Consistently. Take care to develop both surprise and speed of execution, as well force delivery. A large heavy boxing bag can assist in this.

3.3. Don't attempt an Entry whilst the Opponent is moving backwards or dancing with you. Entries are most effective on stationary or forward moving Opponents. There is thus a strong timing element to the effective use of the entry.

4. **WHEN TO TRANSITION**: Immediately once positive pressure has been established. The two main elements that hamper positive pressure are the following: One, the Opponent wedging a limb in between the participant's bodies. In this case the limb needs to be dealt with either by redirecting it or by the Trainee moving their body. And two, the Opponent's body starting to move backwards. In this case consider the aptness of striking, going for Control, or disengaging.

CONTROL

1. **GOAL DEFINITION**: Neutralizing the immediate threat through

controlling its movement.

2. **GOAL INSIGHT**:

2.1. The main outcome is ensuring the Opponent's weapon is unable to damage you. The easiest way to accomplish is to simply be out of range. However, in a CCI, this not possible. Therefore we need to be close enough to control the movement of the weapon. This could mean controlling the weapon hand or arm, but can possibly mean controlling the Opponent's complete body as well.

2.2. Control does not necessarily equate to a lack of movement in either Trainee or Opponent. It predominantly means lack of movement of certain limbs or parts of the body. The rest of the body, as well as the collective bodies of the participants, may still be moving very dynamically. Either way, the weapon movement has been halted or hampered in such a way that it cannot damage the Trainee.

2.3. This phase of the CCI should set up the Opponent for the Takedown. As we gain Control the CCI stabilises for a moment or two. Somewhere in this segment of the CCI, between gaining Control and stabilising, a pass or position change of either the Opponent or the Trainee should be affected. This pass or positioning is the setup for the Takedown. At it's simplest form this means affecting a break in the Opponent's structural integrity and/or to start moving their centre of gravity outside their base.

3. **PRO TIPS**:

3.1. Don't hang around in Control. There is a threshold over which the Opponent will start to adapt to your movement. If you want to retain initiative you always need to operate under this threshold. When practicing the Control Goal Trainees tend to stay there longer than necessary. This is fine initially as it's necessary to program System 1, however, Trainees should manage the reduction of time spent in Control as they progress in competency.

3.2. Constantly develop your Situational Awareness in Control. The issue at hand is to be sensitive for changes in your Opponent's structure or movement patterns. This sensitivity forms part of your Continuous Assessment discipline. It is necessary to develop this discipline as it will help you to discover moments in which you can either pass the

Opponent, or otherwise transition to a joint lock, in preparation for the Takedown.

3.3. Manipulate your own body, not that of your Opponent. When in Control the skill is to attach yourself to your Opponent, not to try and manipulate their bodies. It might very well be that your Opponent is physically larger or stronger than you, or of a state of mind that will make it difficult to physically Control them through strength alone. Rather manage your own body.

3.4. Joint locks can be used either to severely damage as well as to affect Takedowns. Joint locks are used in submission tactics and sports fighting exactly because they are the precursors to severe joint damage. Context and outcome should influence how and to what extent you apply a joint lock. If necessary don't hesitate to destroy a joint.

4. **WHEN TO TRANSITION**: During the pass or positioning of your Opponent's body there will be a moment where his movement, structure or balance has been compromised. The Takedown needs to feed from this moment. This will ensure the maximum odds of achieving a successful Takedown as you are capitalizing on your Opponent's own momentum.

TAKEDOWN

1. **GOAL DEFINITION**: The act of putting the Opponent on the floor.

2. **GOAL INSIGHT**:

2.1. Self explanatory.

3. **PRO TIPS**:

3.1. Takedowns deployed should be robust and focused on the Opponent's gross movement patterns. For every gross movement pattern one primary Takedown should be selected and trained. Slight variations in the application for the Takedown can be incorporated but the main movement patterns of the Takedown shouldn't change much through any of the variations selected.

3.2. Takedowns should be executed with extreme commitment. i.e. as hard and as fast as possible. Someone once said that you can never hit faster than gravity or harder than the ground. Most of the times when we fall we have a certain amount of control over that fall. We don't necessarily realise that we do, but we do. Our brains prioritise balance above most things so it is extremely aware of slipping, skidding and falling. If it senses the fall it will automatically try an autocorrect and frequently it will send out a limb to try and buffer the fall. Falling as dead weight, at speed, and with no protection, is a different ball game. It is extremely painful and can be very damaging. This is the reason many traditional and sport fighting arts develop good falling technique. We want to capitalize on this potential disruption and incapacitation by putting our Opponents down faster than which their brains can intervene. We also want to use as much force in the Takedown as we can, bearing in mind again that context and desired outcome should influence our decisions here.

3.3. Learn to adjust your range as your Opponent goes down. After the Takedown we again want to transition into a form of Control so that we can apply whatever Finish Technique or Procedure we need to. If the Finish movement requires a medium (arm length) to close (elbow length) range you want to be in that range the moment your Opponent hits the ground. This requires that you actively adjust the range as your Opponent is falling. Conversely, if your Opponent has to fall on your feet with his weight pressing against your lower legs you will lose balance as your center of gravity gets driven over your trapped base. In this case you will also need to adjust range, albeit away from your Opponent rather than towards.

4. **WHEN TO TRANSITION**: The moment that your Opponent loses balance and starts to fall the Trainee should be adjusting range to ensure balance integrity and setting up the Finish. Transitioning into the Finish is very dependent on the Finish itself. In a self defense situation Finish might be a last strike to back of the neck, in this case the priority would be disengaging, ranging accurately, and waiting for the opportunity to strike the Opponent. In an LEO environment Finish might be affecting an arrest, in this case it would be highly beneficial to retain Control of the Opponent's closest arm during the fall and to range according to that. Control of the arm would mean faster manipulation of the Opponent's body weight once they hit the floor. In a military environment Finish might be disengaging, ranging to a safe distance to drawing a side arm, and firing at the Opponent. In all of these situations the Opponent's fall is the moment when we start to transition, but the outcome highly influences where we transition to.

FINISH

1. **GOAL DEFINITION**: The final action taken to reach the desired outcome in terms of resolving the CCI.

2. **GOAL INSIGHT**:

2.1. The Finish is highly dependent on the desired outcome of the Trainee. Possible desired outcomes may be escaping, stopping an attack, affecting an arrest, in legally justifiable contexts it might even be killing. Techniques and Procedures should be selected and trained specifically for the context and the desired outcome of the Trainees.

3. **PRO TIPS**:

3.1. Train Finish Techniques just as much as any other Techniques. There is no one Goal in the Process that is more or less important than the other. Training time should be given equally to each of the Goals. The risk, because Finish is the last Goal, is to either skip or rush it. However, in certain contexts the Finish is the most important and can easily become one of the most complex Goals. An apt example would be LEOs needing to affect arrests. We have frequently seen training environments glancing over this part of the Process to the extreme detriment of their officers.

3.2. Remember to follow through on Finish Techniques. The fundamental of follow through comes from the shooting environment. When we follow through it means that we are spending enough time observing the situation to ensure that we have actually reached the desired outcome. We do not have to spend more time than necessary to make the accurate judgment call, but we need to spend enough time to make an accurate judgment call. If, for whatsoever reason, the Trainee has not followed through, affecting a completed Finish, the risk is there that the CCI will simply restart.

4. **WHEN TO TRANSITION**: The moment that the desired outcome has been reached disengagement can be considered.

CCI PROCESS PRINCIPLES

There are specific principles that guide us in the resolution of the CCI. These principles should guide Goal achievement during the Process. They are as follows:

1. **ALWAYS manage balance**. We have discussed this but we would just like to note it again. It's a fundamental need of movement and survival; its importance cannot be overemphasized.

2. **Focus should be on achieving the Goals, not on Techniques**. After studying the Process you should notice that there is a glaring lack of Techniques. This does not mean Techniques aren't important, but they are only a means to an end. To be honest, any Technique that fits the descriptions found anywhere within this book can be selected and trained. As long as it gets the job done as fast and as effectively as possible. It's also important to the authors that this process can be adopted regardless of what background the Trainee comes from. Feel free to test Techniques you are comfortable with for efficacy within the Process. We tell our Trainees that Techniques are tools, and that we can teach them many tools, but our responsibility is to teach them how to get the job done. Furthering this analogy, if they need an extra tool in their toolbox to get the job done then great, we'll teach them. But the idea is not for them to lug a heavy and cluttered toolbox, with a bunch of tools they don't really need, around to every job.

3. **Each Goal should be achieved as fast as possible.** At no stage do we want to give the Opponent an opportunity to adapt to what we are doing. We want to retain initiative at all times and force him to react to our movements. This means we want to transition to a next Goal or movement before his brain can identify what we are doing and start to actively resist or pick an appropriate defense.

4. **Aim to apply enough force to stop the attack immediately every time you progress to a next Goal**. Whether launching an Entry, applying a joint lock in Control or doing a Takedown, you should attempt to stop the attack each time you transition into one of these Goals. This is as much a mindset issue as it is a Technique or Tactic issue. The faster you resolve the CCI by stopping your Opponent the less risk you are exposed to. Treat the transition into every Goal as an opportunity to incapacitate, albeit not necessarily severely damage or critically injure, your Opponent. The extent of the damage needs to be determined by the context and desired outcome of the CCI.

5. **Do not relinquish ground if not completely necessary.** You should almost never disengage or relinquish Control if you don't absolutely have to. Trainees should condition themselves to drive forward and through the Process. They should aggressively hunt and work for the next Goal, and then the next Goal, and then the next, continuing to do so until they reach Finish and the CCI has been resolved. Relinquishing Control is especially risky if it allows the Opponent to start using their weapon again and should only be done if there is absolutely no other means of moving the Process forward.

6. **The first fight is for Control, the second fight is to Finish.** When the CCI launches, all of the Trainee's focus and energy should go into achieving Control. That would include any and/or all elements of Assess, managing the initial attack and avoiding immediate injury, the Entry, gaining Control, and stabilizing the CCI for the moment or two needed to transition to the Takedown. This part of the CCI forms a very natural unit, as do the Takedown and the Finish. It is also a mindset issue as it forces the Trainee into not skipping Goals. Trainee injury or death most frequently occurs when there is no clear drive or Tactics towards Control. When Control is lacking the weapon is still in play and the Opponent can essentially continue to damage the Trainee. As such, we want to ensure that the Trainee first addresses the weapon before progressing to the Takedown and Finish.

7. **The purpose of Disrupting is to ensure compliance.** We train and deploy selected martial arts or combative techniques specifically to Disrupt our Opponent. In very basic terms the CNS is like a water pipe. It has a specific volume of water, or data or information then, which it can transport or store in any single moment. If we had to connect a high pressure air pump to the water pipe we can blow the water out of the pipe with the air. In close combat then, when we apply enough force, whether by causing pain or damage, or alternatively just transferring kinetic energy, it's like "high pressure air" that blows the existing data or information out of the CNS "water pipe." This is what we call Disrupting. The effect of the Disruption is to cause a stutter in the Opponent's functioning, a moment or more of compliance. It is in these moments that we transition to the next Goal. If the Opponent is already compliant then no Disruption is necessary.

8. **If stuck, maintain Control, reassess Assess, and adapt accordingly**. We have touched on this dynamic previously in the section on Continuous Assessment drills. In practice the Trainee needs to be conditioned to lock Control in and ensure they can maintain it for the time needed to Assess.

CHAPTER THIRTEEN: TECHNIQUES, DRILLS AND TRAINING SESSIONS

STANCE

Start from feet under the hips and take then take one comfortable step forward. Be careful not to travel the forward stepping foot to the body's centre line. It should move straight forward, not forward and in. If it does travel slightly in, it shouldn't go further in than what it would travel should the Trainee be walking. We frequently put a straight line indicator under the stepping foot to assist. The step forward is on the empty hand side keeping the weapon side to the back. The idea is to stick to as natural a position as possible, avoiding very deep, wide or complicated stances whilst still providing some stance integrity.

Arms are tight to the side. When in interview stance the hands are side by side, not holding, and no fingers interlocked. In fighting stance the open hand is slightly in front of the weapon hand. To find the perfect arm position, fully extend arms forward and place palms vertically against each other. This is what's called the power triangle. From this position simply drop the elbows straight down and to the sides of the body lightly making contact with the sides of the ribs. Again, as above, the idea is to find a comfortable position that your body knows very well. The Torso faces the Opponent almost squarely.

As a last note, and entirely up to the Trainee, if the Trainee is completely new to edge and point work (or if the Trainee is a good learner), and the Trainee will be carrying and using firearms, we encourage them to consider starting their edged and pointed work from the side that will not primarily be gripping their firearm. The learning curve will only be a bit slower but it will open up future carry and accessing options.

Foot Position

Power Triangle

Fighting Stance

Folded Arms Stance 1

Folded Arms Stance 2

DIVE ENTRY

The Dive Entry is our standard entry Technique deployed for closing range. It's a compound gross motor movement that, when executed correctly, delivers an immense amount of force via it's striking component. It's called the Dive Entry as Trainees' hands and arms resemble a dive in the starting position.

The elbows are bent to around 135º, pointing downwards (not out), and kept tightly close to the side (think Live in the Box from the Ten Principles of The Maul). The hands are open but close together, fingers pointing forward, and are aimed simply to the left or right of the Opponent's head, the determining factor being the Opponent's weapon side. Contact is made with the forearms and the top forearm is aimed at the neck, ideally connecting with the throat or the side of the neck. In training control for safety and land the Dive Entry on the same angle but a couple of inches lower than the neck on the upper torso. The bottom arm intercepts the Opponent's weapon arm and provides positive pressure to it. The angle of the Opponent's weapon arm will influence the angle on the Trainee's bottom arm. This Technique can be used with or without the Trainee's weapon in hand; literally nothing changes in the execution.

Care should be taken not to immediately "catch" the Opponent (grabbing the Opponent's neck, shoulder or arms) when the Dive Entry is used offensively. When used offensively the Dive Entry is first and foremost an impact strike. After the strike's force has been delivered, and the Opponent's gross movement pattern allows for the Trainee to purposefully transition into Control, should the hands transition from diving hands into grabbing hands. When used defensively the Dive Entry strongly resembles a flinch response, the main difference being the fact that the Dive and its striking component can't be set up in time. In this case simply let the arms travel up and intercept the Opponent. The top arm should still aim to cover the area from the Opponent's neck downwards, the bottom arm should still intercept the weapon arm. If possible still make contact with the forearms. The Trainee's interjecting elbow and shoulder joints will act as shock absorbers to the incoming force. Once contact has been made take care to adjust the feet for balance. The best is to ingrain a slight shuffle into most end of range lower body movement patterns, this shuffle will allow System 1 to automatically control for balance.

In offensive and defensive use respectively, aim the bottom arm to strike or intercept the Opponent's weapon arm's bicep area, thus in the center of the Opponent's upper arm.

To teach the perfect position and range start from contact and reverse engineer. What we mean by this, is let the Trainee get into the perfect contact position, placing their forearms in the exact locations on the Opponent's body where they want to make contact. After the arms and torso are set, let the Trainee fix his feet into a perfectly balanced fighting stance. From that position let them take one comfortable step backwards and relax the arms into a natural interview stance.

Step 1.

Step 2.

Step 3.   Step 4.

Initial System 2 based training has to include the above exercise (which we call Ranging). Ranging is the process of determining the perfect range for the Technique we want to practice. Before we start a repetition we will literally tell the Trainee to first Range. After they have Ranged, we will execute the Technique. These two steps, first Range and second execute, will be followed until the Trainee automatically Ranges correctly.

Lastly, the Dive Entry is launched from a Drop Step. A Drop Step is a controlled fall using gravity to accelerate body movement and placing as much mass, at as much acceleration possible, behind the strike. The Drop Step starts the power generation on the rear foot and feeds into an end of movement snap of the forearms. Remind the Trainee to the shift body weight to the rear leg the moment the Trigger containing the Dive Entry as Move has been set.

TETHERING

Tethering is a method of controlling the Opponent through positive pressure and without having to apply a strict joint lock. It's highly dependent on positive pressure though and it shouldn't be attempted when the Opponent is dancing with you, or when the Opponent is back peddling faster than at which you can maintain balance integrity.

Although Tethering can be applied wherever positive pressure is present, let's discuss it primarily as follow up to the Dive Entry. Presupposing that the Dive Entry has not immediately incapacitated the Opponent, and safe application of positive pressure is possible, the first step would be to grab the Opponent with the hands. The second step is to collapse into the Opponent, completely bending the elbows and getting as close as possible. Feet should be brought close to the Opponent to account for balance integrity. When collapsing, the Trainee should wedge their bottom elbow in between the Opponent's weapon arm and torso, stopping the Opponent's weapon arm from slipping underneath the Tether. The extreme close range will provide three main benefits:

1. The Trainee will have the maximum tactile feedback and subsequently the fastest response time.

2. The Trainee should be in a range that will make it difficult for the Opponent to use the weapon.

3. The Trainee will be better positioned to Transition into a Control joint lock or a Takedown.

In this Tethered position the Trainee needs to practice three main outcomes:

1. **Moving with and staying extremely close to the Opponent**. Simply let the Opponent move around dynamically and let the Trainee work to maintain the positive pressure.

2. **Managing the Opponent's weapon arm**. Let the Opponent move the weapon arm up, down, to the sides, backwards and forwards and let the Trainee work to maintain the positive pressure. As the Trainee becomes more adept let the Opponent actively try and get the arm out of the Tether to assist System 1's conditioning.

3. **Passing the Tether into a joint lock or a Takedown**. Care should be taken that the Trainee is consistently applying Continuous Assessment (through tactile feedback). The Trainee should be sensitive for moments where the Opponent's momentum or movement patterns are providing good opportunity for passing the Tether. The Trainee should not be forcing the pass as they are not guaranteed they will be able to physically manipulate a non compliant Opponent outside of the training environment.

As discussed previously the idea is not to hang around in Control. However, the three outcomes above need to be practiced. Therefore we suggest having a set amount of repetitions where the Trainee can focus on the list above, and a set amount of repetitions where the Trainee is encouraged to pass the Tether as fast as possible making sure not to compromise any of the above outcomes.

| TETHERING | TETHERING - LOW | TETHERING - HIGH |

THE OPEN ARM AND HAND

Effective use of the open arm extends to four main functions. For ease of remembrance we refer to them as the Four Ds.

1. **Distract.** Any Technique specifically used to distract the Opponent. Primarily deployed before the CCI phase of any situation. It might be the Trainee pointing behind the Opponent and saying "watch out" or "there's police there." It might be taking something out of their pockets drawing the Opponent's eyes down. Regardless of the trick employed, the idea is that the weapon and weapon hand stays free to either strike or access.

2. **Deflect.** In The Maul deflection is primarily via Trapping and will be discussed below.

3. **Disrupt**. The act of applying force to an Opponent with the goal of gaining their compliance. This concept has already been discussed. In relation to the open arm and hand though we will encourage the Trainee to be creative in its use. Not flashy, stupid or complicated, simply to work beyond standard striking patterns. A hand in the face. A hand grabbing the cheeks, eyes or ears. A choking hand. A hand grabbing the Opponents' testicles and either squeezing or pulling them. Any and all of these will achieve the same goal of Disrupting.

4. **Disengage**. In The Maul disengagement is primarily focused on stripping an Opponent's grab hand off the Trainee's weapon arm and will be discussed below. In any outcome where disengagement before the Takedown is needed or beneficial, disengagement would be shoving the Opponent away after passing the Tether.

TAKEDOWNS

We have purposefully decided not to discuss Takedowns in the book for two main reasons.

First of all, anybody coming from an existing martial art or combative background will already be schooled in certain Takedowns. Takedowns are complex movement patterns that take time to perfect. There is enough information in the previous chapter to assist readers in selecting Takedowns that will be appropriate in the Process and we want to encourage them to test their existing repertoire in this regard.

Secondly, for those that do not have an existing repertoire, and because of the issue of complexity, it is honestly very difficult to teach or learn Takedowns on written media. If you need examples or training in this regard feel free to reach out directly to the authors.

CHAOS DRILLS

Apart from the first three access drills, which form the foundation of some of the other drills, most of these drills have specifically been selected and/or developed to increase performance in System 1. The intention is to take the *flailing of the arms* and to weaponize them. None of the Chaos Drills should be scripted or controlled; they should be treated as either Unscripted Training or Play Learning. They can be assigned starting points and possibly outcomes.

1. ACCESS DRILLS. The Access drills allow us to practice getting our knife into play. Access drills should initially be practiced from a relaxed stance, transitioning from a comfortable cluster into a fighting stance.

1.1. ACCESSING PROCEDURE

1.1.1. **Move arms into position**. Let the brain take the shortest route possible into position. Position here denotes right above the weapon for the open hand and ready and close to the handle for the weapon hand.

1.1.2. **Break concealment**. Apart from the One Handed accessing option, the open arm and hand will break concealment. The easiest and fastest way to break concealment is to grab a full hand of the clothing garment immediately above the weapon and lift. The full hand of garment diminishes the need for accuracy and assists where full fine motor movement has diminished. Lifting from right above the weapon assures that we only need to move the shortest movement distance, it also assists that the clothing doesn't catch on the weapon (something that frequently happens when breaking concealment from below the weapon). When accessing with one hand the same principles are followed, the only difference being that it would now be the weapon hand breaking concealment.

1.1.3. **Draw**. Working slow and controlled, make sure that the Trainee is gripping the knife properly before drawing. Special emphasis should be placed on this as it's one of the elements that regresses the most when working at speed. Initially train and practice sequentially in System 2. Mentally follow the pattern: Perfect Grip. Perfect Draw. Let speed come alongside accuracy of movement. Encourage the Trainee to develop an index in their grip that will indicate to them that the grip is correct. When drawing the weapon make sure the movement is away from the abdomen and into the stance so as not to cut themselves.

1.2. **ACCESSING POSITIONS**. In all three of these positions first train accessing whilst in a good fighting stance. After this can be done smoothly and at speed progress to the other drills listed in 1.3. below.

1.2.1. **Interview Stance**. Open arm side foot to the front, weapon side foot to the back; fighting stance but with hands in front and side by side. Access from this position.

1.2.2. **Arms Folded**. Feet and body position as above. Open arm side horizontally against the body - think arms folded position with this arm underneath. Weapon arm either loosely over the open arm as in proper arms folded position or bent 90 º up with the hand on the chin as in a reflective position. This position is purposed to look less obvious. Access from this position.

1.2.3. **One Hand**. Feet, body and arm positions can vary, although there is value in initially training from the basic fighting foot position. Break concealment with the same hand that will be accessing.

Interview Stance   **Accessing**

1.3. TRANSITION INTO STANCE WHILST ACCESSING DRILLS.

1.3.1. **Access in Process**. In this drill the Trainee is already in Process. It might be that they've affected an Entry, or that they are busy fighting for Control, they might even have put the Opponent on the floor, regardless, have them access the weapon in Process.

1.3.2. **Agility drill**. Have the Trainee move around the training environment at increasing speed. They can run, shuffle laterally, fall and stand up, basically whatever movement you can come up with, and have them access and transition into fighting stance somewhere mid movement but on your command or using the Ready drill variation below. This drill will assist greatly in balance development. If the Trainee struggles with balance teach them to always add two to three short shuffle steps into their transition as System 1 will automatically use these shuffle steps to fix balance.

1.3.3. **Ready drill**. Have the Trainee stand comfortably. Let them pick a number from 1 - 5 in their minds, they shouldn't communicate the number out loud. The instructor then counts from 1 to 5. When the Trainee hears their number they need to draw their weapon and transition into a fighting stance. There are infinite variations on this drill, but what's important is to understand its function: It trains the ARM Yourself process. Specifically Trigger Setting and the transition from Ready into Move. The Trainee's mental number selection is a Trigger that's been set. i.e. the Trainee made a decision that IF they hear a specific number THEN they will draw their weapon. Listening for the number is Assessing, drawing the weapon is Move. This drill can be used with different tactile stimuli and easily be made more or less complex.

1.3.4. **Ambush drill**. Let the Opponent aggressively assault the Trainee. Attacks should be a surprise, close to full speed, include multiple and consistent stabbing and significant forward pressure. Let the Trainee manage this incoming problem using all the tools at his disposal (moving, trapping, Dive Entry etc), whilst working for the opportunity to draw.

2. THE MAUL FLOW DRILL.

2.1. MOVEMENT PRINCIPLES

2.1.1. **Snappy stabs**. Stabs should accelerate towards the target, the actual weapon and wrist moving faster than the fore and upper arm. The stab should snap in and out making sure to close the elbow when retracting.

2.1.2. **Large cuts**. End all stabs with drags of the blade to enlarge the laceration. This can be accomplished either by moving the arm or just the wrist.

2.1.3. **Move at the elbow**. When retracting the weapon arm we do so by closing the elbow and not by pulling the weapon towards us. It essentially means that we pull the stab away and out instead of backwards. The two main reasons for this is one, to stop the blade from getting stuck, and two, to stop the Trainee from stabbing themselves in the stomach or chest area.

2.1.4. **Piston action**. Probably one of the most important skills to develop is that of keeping both the Trainee's arms in play. We do so through creating a piston action rhythm where the hands pass each other around the middle of the movement pattern. The open hand travels over the retracting weapon arm and its energy is towards the front. If you are the instructor you will probably need to shout something like both arms at your Trainees until they get used to it. Once System 1 has grabbed a hold of it though, it happens extremely naturally.

2.1.5. **Do massive damage.** Remember that The Maul is directed chaos. The piston action should be used to stab and cut each and every target that presents itself. To do so consistently and extremely violently without pausing or dueling. Do enough damage, fast enough, to demotivate or incapacitate the Opponent as fast as possible.

Start...

...Finish

2.2. **FOUR MAIN LINES.** The first three lines being Forward, Outside and Inside, can be visualized as 12, 3 and 9 (3 and 9 not necessarily respectively, as it's determined by the Trainee's weapon hand) on an analogue clock, the elbow being the center of the clock. Most other lines of attack, including the Two Extra Lines, are mere variations of the Four Main Lines.

2.2.1. **Line 1: Forward.** A stab straight to the front. Imagine dragging the tip from the Opponent's forehead to their chin. The Trainee's elbow should have moved closer to his centre line to ensure staying behind the blade

2.2.2. **Line 2: Outside.** A diagonal or angled stab, into the neck area.

Imagine sticking the knife into the side of the neck at a 45º angle. Outside denotes the Opponents left side if the Trainee is right handed and vice versa. The Trainee's elbow should have moved closer to his centre line to ensure staying behind the blade

2.2.3. **Line 3: Inside**. A diagonal or angled stab, into the neck area. Imagine sticking the knife into the side of the neck at a 45º angle. Inside denotes the Opponents right side if the Trainee is right handed and vice versa. The Trainee's elbow should have moved closer to his centre line to ensure staying behind the blade.

2.2.4. **Line 4: Horizontal**. A stab where the forearm is parallel to the floor, from the outside to the inside. Imagine grabbing an Opponent in close from the front and stabbing him in the kidneys. The Trainee's elbow should be closer to the same side of his torso.

Line 1 – Forward

Line 2 - Outside

Line 3 – Inside

Line 4 – Horizontal

2.3. **TWO EXTRA LINES**. Some have asked why we separate these two lines from the other four. Predominantly it's for simplicity sake - we want to give System 1 as much time to learn and condition with as few movements as possible. Essentially these two lines are variations of Line 4 and so the main movement patterns are initially practiced as a unit there.

2.3.1. **Line 5: Low Outside**. A low but upwards jerking stab, anywhere close to center line and from the femoral arteries to the abdomen. Outside denotes the Trainees weapon tip pointing to the outside, for a right handed Trainee the tip would be pointing up and right and vice versa for a left-handed Trainee. The Trainee's elbow should be somewhere between the same side of the torso to centre line.

2.3.2. **Line 6: Low Inside**. A low but upwards jerking stab, anywhere close to centre line and from the femoral arteries to the abdomen. Inside denotes the Trainee's blade tip pointing to the inside, for a right handed Trainee the tip would be pointing up and left and vice versa for a left-handed Trainee. The Trainee's elbow should be somewhere between the same side of the torso to centre line.

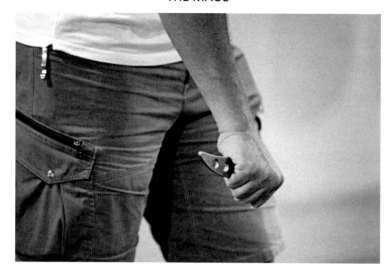

Line 5 – Low Outside

Line 6 – Low Inside

3. **BUILDING THE FLOW**.

   3.1. Repeat a Line individually. Pick one of the Lines and repeat it 10x times sequentially.

3.2. Repeat all Four Lines as a super set. Sequentially repeat the Four Main Lines as 4x sets of 10x repetitions.

3.3. Occasionally add the Two Extra Lines.

3.4. Repeat sets of the Four Main Lines where the Lines are not sequentially linear, use the following principles to assist in development:

3.4.1. Left to Right, High to Low. When attacking on a specific angle or line, the Opponent's System 1 will send a defensive movement in the general direction from which the attack is coming (albeit using a probability algorithm). If the Trainee keeps attacking on that line the Opponent's brain will eventually become more accurate at dealing with the attack. Better to learn to switch angles and Lines naturally to the opposite sides of where the Opponent is focusing defense. The idea here is not to ingrain combinations but to develop System 1's ability to switch between the Lines on impulse.

3.4.2. Add Torso Movement. After the Trainee becomes adept at the lines (which shouldn't take very long) start adding in movement on the torso. The torso can only go forwards, backwards, left, right, high and low. The Trainee should play with adding each of these movements (randomly) to the different line. For example. Time can be spent in Line 1 alone but moving the torso around, or time can be spent with the torso left but moving through all the Lines. After a while completely random combinations of torso movement and Line execution should be encouraged. Again, the focus is on creating diverse but natural movement patterns in and for System 1 and not necessarily on combinations.

3.4.3. Add Foot Movement. Lastly, as above, foot movement can be added into the mix. It doesn't really matter what foot movement patterns gets utilized. Adhering to the principles of managing balance primarily through smaller more frequent steps, as well as avoiding large and complicated transitions, is important though. Other than that the emphasis should simply be on moving and Flowing.

4. **FLOW TRAINING**. Trainee and Opponent practicing Flowing, Trapping and

Striking on each other. Both Trainee and Opponent are learning and practicing at the same time.

5. **ACCESS & FLOW.** A combination of an Access Drill combined with a short flow (two to three strikes).

6. **ACCESS & STRIKE.** A combination of an Access Drill and one targeted strike. Have the Trainee pick a target within their sight picture. It can be anything that their eyes can lock onto. Trainees can be placed facing each other, but at a distance, using each other to visualize targets. Alternatively, invest in building or acquiring dummies or strike boards. Strike boards are very affordable and can be home built.

7. **TRAPPING.** Trapping can best be thought of as a deflection but with longer contact time.

7.1. Traps are executed open handed and they do not immediately grab. A Trap can be transitioned into a grab due to the longer contact time but great care should be taken not to try and immediately grab or catch an attacking forearm or hand when defending. Grabs and catches require a great amount of accuracy and coordination which are simply too difficult to execute well at speed; if System 1 was taught to grab at low speed it will attempt to do so at high speed, and fail. Rather Trap and transition into a grab.

7.2. When Trapping, the hand is almost flat but the fingers are relaxed and slightly curved. The Trap intercepts the incoming limb anywhere from the Trapping hand's fingers and down the forearm to the elbow. The idea is to create a very large Trapping surface to better ensure a successful defense.

7.3. The Trap should never travel far over the Trainee's centre line (think Live in the Box). Traps shouldn't be large or jerky movements. They should literally only travel as far as necessary to avoid being hit, they should be smooth and flowing, they should intercept the incoming attack and not go and fetch it.

7.4. Initially train and practice Trapping with only slight backwards movement. Imagine the Opponent attacking the Trainee whilst moving forward, and the Trainee adapting to the Opponent's movement by moving slightly backwards. This simulates System 1's natural backwards flinch when ambushed. However, as soon as the Trainee has become adept at intercepting this initial attack, start including forward and outside movement driving. The idea is to train not to get stuck in a back peddling loop whilst Trapping, and to transition into a forward drive as soon as the flinch is done.

7.5. Start training slowly and by trapping only one attack movement at a time. Attack speeds and volume can be increased as the Trainee progresses. Attacks should always remain Unscripted. Traps can be to the inside or the outside. 8. Trapping with Knife. Exactly the same as with Trapping but simply using the knife to do the work. The pikal style blade resembles a hand, use it as such.

8. **TRAPPING WITH KNIFE**. Exactly the same as with Trapping but simply using the knife to do the work. The pikal style blade resembles a hand, use it as such.

8.1. Dragging the edge. Develop the habit to drag the edge over the Opponent's body when retracting the knife Trap. Simply adjust the wrist to whatever angle is necessary to do so.

9. **STRIPPING**. In dynamic encounters limbs get stuck. One of the biggest risks the Trainee has is the Opponent grabbing his weapon hand or arm. The Trainee should be conditioned to identify and immediately attend to this problem should it arise. Stripping is the act of removing the Trainee's weapon hand and arm from the Opponent's grip. It's one of the main functions of the open hand and also executes very naturally from the Flow Drill. These are the steps once the Trainee identifies that the Opponent has grabbed his weapon arm:

9.1. Base the feet.

9.2. Place the open hand on the top of the weapon arm.

9.3. Move the open hand down the weapon arm violently striking the Opponent's hand off the weapon arm taking care to jerk the weapon arm away at the same time.

141

9.4. To train this have the Opponent periodically transition a weapon arm Trap into a grab during Flow Training taking care to spend a lot of practice time at System 2 speeds.

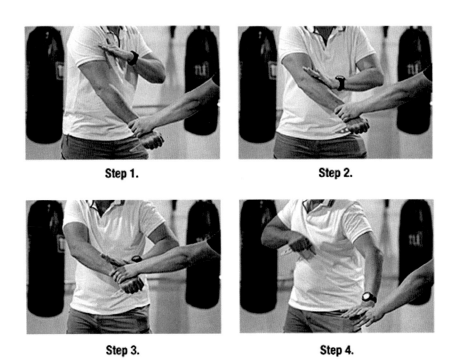

Step 1.   Step 2.

Step 3.   Step 4.

10. **TRAP & STRIKE**. Trainees should always have a mindset of stopping the attack as soon as possible. They should never get stuck in a defensive loop but should be taught to transition from defense to offence as soon as possible. The Trap & Strike drill achieves this outcome. The Opponent launches a single committed attack at the Trainee - being careful to vary his attack every repetition. The Opponent should not get stuck in using the same patterns of attack, or even worse, only using attack patterns learned in The Maul. The Opponent should glean from other styles and systems as the goal in this drill is not for the Opponent to practice, but for the Trainee to learn to adapt to whatever the incoming attack is. The Trainee's goal is to Trap the first attack, move into a position from which they can strike, pick an available target, and then execute strike. Train at System 2 speeds and again, the Opponent should be careful not to consistently employ The Maul's offensive or defensive patterns in the drill.

11. **OPPORTUNITY ENTRY**. Have the Working Group run any drill but instruct the Opponent to periodically open the weapon arm wide enough that the Trainee can launch a Dive Entry into the hole. The training focus here is first on recognition of the opportunity and second on launching a surprising, quick and powerful Dive Entry. There are two primary variations of this drill: In the first variation the Opponent contests the Dive Entry with the open hand and arm, in the second variation there is no contest and the Opponent lets the Trainee into the hole. Train both.

12. **TRAP & ENTRY**. When Trapping to the outside there is a hole that may open up on the Opponent's centre line. Let the Working Group flow but have the Trainee focus on Trapping to the outside whilst waiting and working for the hole. As above the training focus is both on the recognition of the hole as well as the launch of a successful Dive Entry. Again work both scenarios - contested and uncontested.

13. **ONE MOVE DRILL**. We adapted this drill primarily from Rory Miller's Slow Man Drill *[Miller, Rory. Training for Sudden Violence: 72 Practical Drills (p. 19). YMAA Publication Center, Inc.. Kindle Edition.]*

13.1.　　Both the Trainees and Opponents have to slow down their movements to a speed where System 2 can lead the way. This means slower than which they can think and process; they must be able to actively Assess and select options during the movement cycles.

13.2.　　It is Play Learning based. Assign starting positions and select a participant to take the initiative.

13.3.　　Each participant may only make one move at a time and the focus should be on developing a rhythm. One move may include natural compound movements where the lower and upper body are moving together. Natural in and out movement patterns may also be completed (think a stab going forwards and backwards as one movement in the brain). Moves may however not be sequentially strung together.

13.4.　　Take care not to rush or increase the speed of the drill.

13.5.　　This drill provides a chess-like quality where participants can work on Tactics and System 2 can assist in conditioning System 1 on what may or may not work.

143

13.6.   The main variation we use is to incrementally allow speed increases. Tiny increments though. Always remember that one participant may not work faster than the other as it presupposes that that participant is going to be faster outside the training environment; this presupposition carries the real risk of serious injury or death outside the training environment.

CHAOS DRILL VARIATIONS

1. **Vary starting points**. Starting points relate to different levels as well as positions in relation to objects. Levels can be standing, on the knees, on one knee, on the floor lying down etc. Starting can be free standing, against a wall, in between vehicles (or whatever restraining objects are available), at different ranges etc. The idea here is to emulate different positions that the Trainee might find themselves in during an actual CCI. Thus, don't be weird or silly, keep it accurate.

2. **Alter training speeds**. At the most fundamental level the slowest point on the spectrum would be the fastest speed at which System 2 can comfortably think and make decisions, the fastest point would be an Opponent attacking at full speed (think speed threshold) and relentlessly (think volume threshold). Training can and should be varied along the whole spectrum. Training should also account for fluctuations in speed (think a participant being injured or gassing out) as well as unconventional attack rhythms (think an extremely drunk person just randomly, and sometimes even slowly, swinging a knife at you on a very wide arc).

3. **Change Opponent weapons, quantities, behaviors and motivations**. All of these items can be randomized. Weapon selections should be primarily endemic and should account for different ranges (think short knives vs. Machetes, a reality in Africa and some Asian societies). Opponent quantities can either be static or extra Opponents can be introduced as the CCI develops. Opponents can assist by emulating drunks, tweakers (tik koppe), pain resistance, assassins, robbers, emotionally unstable individuals etc.

4. **Change the environment and/or train in different environments**. If the actual environment can't be changed (think the beach, parks, nature,

public transport, toilets or other rooms or facilities, parking lots or garages, vehicles) objects can be strewn around the training floor. The training space can also be restricted (think assigning a 4 sqm block in which the Working Group has to fight). The idea here is to develop awareness of the environment during the CCI. Very practically, if the Trainee does not remain environmentally aware they might trip and stumble or fall, they might also miss the introduction of extra Opponents. In terms of the restricting space: It's important to understand that when Trainees do not work in different space constraints, they may assume that certain movements or Techniques will work in a space where they actually will not.

5. **Lastly, vary applicable drill starting positions between weapons accessed and not accessed.** Do so for both the Trainee and the Opponent. The Trainee should be just as adept at accessing from any variation as Assessing within any variation. The Trainee should be able to identify when an Opponent attempts to access a weapon and then to adapt accordingly.

TRAINING SESSIONS

TRAINING SESSION PRINCIPLES

1. **Emulate actual CCIs.** Always make sure that training remains relevant to an actual CCI. The primary concern is emulating realistic sections, events and movement cycles within a CCI. Don't waste time on peripheral, weird or silly things. If it's not going to help you reach the next Goal in the Process, drop it.

2. **Run drills at speeds that favor both System 2 and System 1.** As frequently discussed, make sure training sessions purposefully include both.

3. **Always establish who's practicing before starting.** When there is a dedicated defender, or starter, the Working Group should establish and indicate who it is before starting. This is simply a safety precaution to ensure no one hits or stabs a participant by accident.

4. **Have a clear "stop" and "freeze" protocol in place.** All participants should be taught to immediately "stop" and disengage on a stop command, and to stop movement BUT NOT disengage on a "freeze" command. It's important to note that participants will most probably experience a level of auditory exclusion during training. The instructor should continue to give the order until it has been adhered to.

5. **Trainee's speed has to be equal to or slower than the Opponent's.** The moment that the Trainee is moving faster than the Opponent during training there is an unconscious assumption that the Trainee will be moving faster than the Opponent in an actual CCI. In all instances where speed is controlled the Opponent should be the controlling agent, the Trainee should match or drop below the Opponent's speed.

POSSIBLE SESSION STRUCTURE

1. **The Maul Flow Drill.**

    1.1. 5 Minutes.

2. **Accessing Drills.**

    2.1. 10 Minutes.

3. **Two to Three Chaos Drills.**

    3.1. 10 - 15 Minutes.

    3.2. Unscripted Training. If participants are brand new Scripted Training will be necessary.

4. **Chaos Drills Variations.**

    4.1. 10 - 15 Minutes.

    4.2. Unscripted Training.

5. The Process, Situations, Play Learning or One Move Drill.

    5.1. 15 - 25 Minutes.

    5.2. Unscripted Training or Play Learning.

CHAPTER 14: THE COMBATIVE EDGE & POINT

THE PIKAL STYLE

If you are unfamiliar with combative edged weapons or defensive knives in general, then the question of "what should I carry?" can be quite an overwhelming one. There are literally thousands of options out there, from relatively inexpensive factory-made knives to purpose built custom knives which can cost quite a lot. Setting aside your budgetary constraints, let's quickly discuss the style of knife.

This is an area again where there are many options to choose from, and every one of them comes with an array of strong opinions on why it's better or worse than another. That is simply the nature of the circle which surrounds these topics. The Maul however has a very strong emphasis on using techniques which are uniquely suited to what is known as a "Reverse Edge" blade, "Pikal Blade" or sometimes spelt "Pakal". This is a knife that has its primary edge on the spine side of the blade. This kind of knife can be held and used in both forward and reverse grips, but for us, our primary focus is on the reverse grip, with the primary edge facing in. So, this will be our area of focus, and it's our strong recommendation that this is the type of knife you should be investing in as its use offers unparalleled interchangeability with other weapons.

Pikal style knives have their origins in the Filipino knife culture, and the word literally means "To Rip" in the Visayan dialect, so naturally you will find a lot of techniques which are well suited to reverse edge blades in Filipino Martial Arts (FMA) specifically in Pekiti Tirsia Kali, though it can also be found elsewhere. In the early 2000's notable instructors like Craig Douglas and Terry Trahan began talking about the Pikal knife and its uses and pioneered much of the techniques associated with the defensive applications of this style of knife both inside and outside of traditional FMA. More recently personalities like Scott Babb and Ed Calderon have popularized the concept even further via social media, reaching a bigger and wider audience than ever before.

The rise in popularity of the style for defensive applications is down to a couple of points. The way in which the knife works almost guarantees damage to the Opponent. Because the blade's edge is reversed the Opponent's own flinch or limb retraction can cause damage to himself. In other words, if you stab into an Opponent's arm for example, his own reaction of withdrawing the limb will cause a deep laceration as he pulls it into the edge of the blade. This is partly what lends this style of knife to close combatives so well.

Another very valid reason is that the movements associated with Pikal style work are very base movements; Pikal style movement patterns do not require a great deal of cognitive thought. This is not meant to sound derogatory at all, but if you have ever seen two untrained women fight, you will notice what kind of movements we as human's resort to when things begin to break down. Interestingly enough, and not comparing women to primates, but the untrained pummeling striking patterns strongly resemble those of gorillas, chimpanzees and other primates. There is a lot of grabbing, clinging on, pulling of hair or clothing, and pummeling with hammer-fists.

This hammer-fist strike is ingrained in us, it's extremely primitive and requires almost no cognitive thought to execute. The Pikal knife slips into this position and simply turns the hammer-fist into a stab, using the same base instinctive movement pattern. This paired with our ability to pull, or rip using the strongest muscles in our body, that of the posterior chain in our back, make the Pikal knife a really formidable close combative edged weapon.

THE INTERCHANGEABILITY OF WEAPONS

One of the unique aspects of The Maul as a system is that it doesn't demand the use of a specific weapon style. Of course, in an ideal world we would want a purpose made Pikal knife, but if for whatever reason that is not an option where you live, travel or operate, then all is not lost.

There are a few important points concerning edged and pointed weapons to keep in mind.

1. Edged and pointed weapons originated as tools.

2. A tool does a job that your hands cannot.

3. Edged and pointed weapons are not "force multipliers."

4. Edged and pointed weapons are "strike enhancers."

The 4 Lines of The Maul's Flow means the Pikal knife can easily be interchanged for other weapons, or even objects. We will discuss more on improvised weapons later on, but even if your knife is more conventional it doesn't mean that you can't still use the movement patterns described in The Maul.

The cutting lines we use in The Maul will work with both Pikal knives or conventional forward grip knives. The cutting lines taught traditionally for forward grip knives won't necessarily always work with Pikal knives. For this reason we opt to rather use lines of movement and a core weapon which offer the widest options for interchangeability.

THE EDGE & POINT WEAPON

It may perhaps sound a bit elementary to more experienced readers, but it's important to know the difference between an edge and a point, and what they will do and what the expected outcome will be when used.

THE POINT

The point at the tip of your blade is really the business end and what makes a knife a lethal force instrument. The lethality of knives comes primarily from their ability to penetrate.

As human beings there are only a few things we are biologically and evolutionarily unprepared to deal with, and one of those things is penetrative injuries. To put it very plainly, if you want to kill you need to penetrate the body.

A pointed weapon, whether it's a knife, a spear, a sword, the arrow, or even a sharpened stick has been the primary weapon of human warfare and combat for millennia because it was the most effective until bullets, bombs and explosives became more efficient.

The vital functions of the human body are all accessed with penetrative depth; the vital organs, the central nervous system (CNS) and major blood vessels all sit inside the body.

From a combative perspective the penetrative weapon also overcomes other obstacles like heavy clothing, and to some extent depending on the specific blade geometry, can even penetrate through soft armor and/or bone. This is an important factor to consider when making your weapon selection.

THE EDGE

The edge is really a secondary consideration when it comes to the combative application of a knife. Pikal blades in specific do very well at utilizing the edge, but the primary focus is still the point.

Slashing and cutting, though it can produce some very graphic and horrifying wounds, doesn't normally result in lethal endings. The human body is better at coping with cuts than it is with penetrative injuries.

Make no mistake though, an edge can still produce serious damage, even more so in the case of heavier blades like machetes, hatchets or axes. Heavy blades that are designed to chop carry with them the ability to sever deeply or decapitate.

This again is another reason to advocate for Pikal blades, as when used with proper technique can result in deep, long wound channels which are simply devastating. You need to be aware though that even something as simple as a heavy cotton jacket can be effective at stopping cuts from lacerating the person wearing it. Clothing is, and has been, an effective method of protecting against slashing cuts for centuries, just think about armor (essentially clothing).

FIXED BLADE CONSIDERATIONS

A fixed blade is still the option of choice for serious tactical, combative and defensive carry. While folding knives do have their place and have some remarkably innovative and effective locking mechanisms now, a fixed blade is inherently stronger simply because it does not fold. This is a critical element when looking at a knife you will depend on to save your life – you don't want one that has the potential to break in half. While the percentage probability of this happening on a modern folder is very low, it's still higher than that of a fixed blade.

When choosing a knife for combative use there are some universal factors to keep in mind, as well as ones specific to either a fixed blade knife or a folding knife.

1. **Fixed Blade Pros:**

    1.1. Lower risk of mechanical failure in the blade.

    1.2. Generally easier and faster to access, especially under duress.
    1.3. Can be a lot easier, and sometimes more comfortable, to conceal carry.

    1.4. Handles can generally be designed more ergonomic as they don't need to house the blade.

2. **Fixed Blade Cons:**

    2.1. Can be illegal depending on where you live.

    2.2. If you're a smaller person it can be difficult to find something to fit your frame and still be of real combative merit.

    2.3. Even if legal, carrying one can be used against you in legal proceedings as they are often labeled "more deadly" by laymen.

FOLDING BLADE CONSIDERATIONS

If you are choosing a folding blade there are a few considerations which are specific to folders.

The main consideration is going to be the lock which holds the knife open and prevents the blade from closing onto your fingers when used.

There are a few types of locking mechanisms commonly used on folding knives. Some of them are adequate, some are better, and some you want to avoid all together when it comes to combative application. We won't go into detail on every conceivable type of locking mechanism but just cover the ones you're likely to come across. It's important that you test out any locking mechanism, regardless of what mechanism it is, to ensure it won't close with a reasonable amount of force applied to it.

1. **Liner Lock**. This type of locking mechanism is very common and makes use of a leaf spring inside the handle frame to fall into place once the blade is opened, locking it in the open position. On paper this isn't a bad design as it does require an intentional movement to release the lock and close the blade. However, if the knife is used and used often, this locking mechanism can wear down and begin to slip with age. If its quality isn't good to start with, it might even slip right out of the box. You need to test it before you carry it.

2. **Frame Lock.** This type of mechanism is becoming more popular and is somewhat stronger than the liner lock. It has a similar system, but instead of using a separate leaf spring, it makes use of the actual frame of the handle. When you grip the handle the pressure from your hand pushes the frame down and locks the blade on opening. As long as you keep gripping the frame the blade should theoretically not be able to close.

3. **Axis Lock**. This is probably the safest mechanism out there, first seen on Benchmade knives, but most likely similar mechanisms are available in other brands by now. Describing the mechanism in written media is difficult. But it relies on a spring tensioned cross bar which effectively slides into place as the blade opens. The bar needs to be physically pulled back to release the lock and while it is in place it creates a very strong lock.

4. **Friction Lock, Slip Joint, Button Lock & Spine Locks**. We know we will be upsetting some people out there, but we are lumping all of these in the same category because they are not suitable for use in combatives. The locking mechanisms are simply not strong enough or can be easily released by accident. I'm sure there are people out there reading this going "but, my one is…" and that's ok. These are general rules and there are always exceptions. Just make sure it's tested and you are confident

in its ability. You don't win any prizes for using an obscure locking mechanism in your knife. The only thing that matters is that it works.

There are very few folding knives which are made specifically for Pikal use. They do exist but they are rare and can be more expensive than a fixed blade. The Spyderco P'Kal springs immediately to mind. If you are using a folding knife in Pikal grip however, generally you will find that you're using the knife against the locking mechanism. That is, any force enacted on the blade is going to pull the knife open if the lock fails and not close it on your fingers, which is actually a pleasant bonus about using folders in Pikal grip.

If you do use a folding knife that isn't specifically designed for Pikal use, you'll want to ensure two things: One, that the edge is sharpened on the appropriate sides, and that two, you can actually grip it properly in relation to the edge. It's a tricky thing to do because ergonomically you're using it wrong, so finding a folding knife that isn't a Pikal design that works in Pikal grip can be difficult but it's not impossible.

1. **Folding Knife Pros**:

    1.1. Generally smaller and easier to carry in a pocket.

    1.2. Generally considered more utilitarian and mundane by the laymen and lawmakers

2. **Folding Knife Cons**:

    2.1. Can be more difficult to access and deploy

    2.2. Even more difficult to deploy in Pikal grip if it's not a Pikal design

    2.3. Good ones can be quite expensive, even more if it's a custom knife

    2.4. The pocket clip is a dead giveaway to anyone who knows what it means, so you have to think outside the box to conceal them properly

GENERAL CONSIDERATIONS FOR KNIVES

In general, there are some aspects of knives for combative use which are considered critical aspects. Meaning they are of vital importance. Some of these considerations may seem over emphasized, or minor. That is for you to decide. The fact that we are discussing a tool which your life may depend on should warrant that no chance is taken. We want to minimize the potential for failure to its smallest percentage possible, and to do that we have to consider details that some may feel are unimportant.

GRIP

This is probably one of the most critical areas, so much so that it's being put first. You can have the best blade in the world, but it means nothing if you can't hold onto it. The stresses involved in a combative encounter are physical, psychological and physiological, and each of these plays a role.

The adrenaline dump which numbs your fine motor skills will be there, how badly it affects you specifically will vary from person to person based on a number of variables, but it will be there. Concerning the actual physical force of the fight, simply not concentrating hard enough on your grip or having a poor grip design, can cause the knife to be levered from your hand.

Don't compound this issue by choosing a knife that has bad ergonomics. Ergonomics refers to the design of an object or tool and how it is optimized for human use. Is the design shaped properly to comfortably sit in human hands? Many designers fall into the trap of creating strikingly beautifully designs to look at, but which are also quite impractical, or simply not comfortable to use.

The handle of your knife, whether fixed or folding in type, should be free of sharp corners or edges, should be made of a tactile material which naturally feels good in your hand. It shouldn't be abrasive or too soft. You want to be able to clench your hand over the grip tightly and still feel that it is comfortable. If there is any discomfort from the handle poking or protruding into your hand, then it may not be a good fit.

The physical size of the handle is also important. If the handle is too wide, or too fat, you may not be able to close your hand around it properly which will compromise your grip. When holding a knife the tips of your fingers should be just touching the inside of your palm. If there is a gap it means the handle is too big and your grip is compromised, if the handle is too small you may find discomfort in your finger tips which may force you to relax your grip.

This is a very difficult thing to get around especially if your hands are particularly big or small. People who live on the extremes of the size scale will find it difficult to find a knife that fits them perfectly. Going to a reputable custom maker will alleviate this issue for you as they should be able to make it to fit you.

BLADE

The business end of your knife has some considerations too. These will be affected a little bit by your local laws, as well as whether you have a fixed blade or folding knife.

Double edge vs single edge is a consideration that many people get hung up on. There's no real wrong answer when it comes to combative use, as both will perform with no real discernible difference to you. The real thing to take into account here is that single edges are inherently stronger than double edges.

All blades are susceptible to lateral forces, i.e. a force enacted on the flat side of the blade. If you can imagine the tip of the blade stuck in something and you twist the handle. That is lateral force. Single edge blades have much more material (steel) at the point of the blade, even when there is a proper distal taper on the blade. This makes it naturally stronger simply because it has more mass. A double edge will conversely be weaker just because it has less.

Why is it such a big deal? Because that lateral force is something that happens fairly often in a combative encounter. It's something you specifically try to avoid when using a knife for any other task (you never pry with a knife for that reason), but in a combative encounter your blade is very likely going to hit bone at some point, and in that moment you won't necessarily have either the control or positioning that allows you to ensure that twisting doesn't take place.

A blade with a naturally reinforced tip will survive it better. If you're getting a knife custom made however, you would have more scope for ensuring this doesn't become a problem. There are a lot of factors from a technical perspective which influence the strength of a blade including the steel used, the edge geometry, the heat treating, and even the way it was made. Reputable high end brands and good custom knife makers will be able to ensure you get a blade that won't fail in its purpose.

Where a double edge does excel over a single edge is simply versatility. With an edge on both sides of the blade the knife can also be used functionally in more conventional styles. This can be a big consideration when you understand that nothing is ever perfect in a combative encounter and you may not have the option of drawing your knife in your preferred hand, or grip. It does also aid in penetration, technically speaking, as the blade is cutting both edges of the entry channel it will naturally penetrate much more easily. However, that has honestly never been a big concern for me.

When you are putting anywhere from 20 kg to 25 kg of mass behind a strike, that energy gets concentrated into an astronomical amount of force when focused on the point of a blade - even a single edge. You really don't need a lot of force to get penetration.

EDGE GEOMETRY

Still on the blade but a little more in depth, the blade geometry refers to the actual edge of the blade and without getting too technical, there are a variety of ways an edge can be put on a blade. Some edge types are better suited for specific tasks.

When you understand the knife making process and specifically when it comes to edge geometry, you understand that everything about a knife is a trade-off. If you want more of one specific feature, it usually comes at the cost of another. You want it to be really sharp? Then you're going to sacrifice some robustness.

 The following assessments are again general. There are a lot of other variables like steel type, heat treating and actual maker's skill which can go into getting an edge geometry that is desired.

There are three main edge types most commonly used in the making of knives.

1. **Hollow grind:**

    1.1. A hollow grind produces a very sharp, but fine edge. This is the type of edge most likely to be on any factory-made knife as from a manufacturing perspective it is easier to make and control. It also produces that hair popping edge that the majority of people want in a knife. But it comes at the cost of being quite fine, and therefore not very robust.

    1.2. A hollow ground edge is more likely to chip or roll when coming into contact with harder materials because it doesn't have the mass to support the edge as much as other grind types do.

2. **Flat or v-grind**:

    2.1. As its name suggests, if you looked at a cross section of a blade with this type of grind it would look like a V. This is a more robust edge than a hollow grind and offers a good middle ground between the very sharp and very robust.

    2.2. Typically, you don't find this type of grind in a factory made knife.

3. **Convex grind**:

    3.1. The convex grind is the most robust of the three. It keeps the most material in supporting the edge and is therefore stronger, but the thickness at the edge can result in a duller blade. That does not mean it cannot be sharp though. Traditionally Japanese swords like Katana also have convex edges, however they also do have a lot more mass behind their cuts to push the blade through material. The convex edge and the extra mass supporting it are what allow that razor sharp sword blade to cut through tatami in one clean motion without dulling.

    3.2. A properly done convex edge can be a beautiful thing, though these edges are generally found more on utilitarian and outdoor knives, which are more general in purpose and need to be a bit more robust.

4. **Hybrid geometry**:

    4.1. In some cases especially with custom knife makers, it is possible to have two types of grinds in a single blade. A double edge, with a flat ground Pikal edge on the one side and a convex conventional edge on the other, can add some mass to the point of a blade giving it some added strength. Or, a reinforced convex point with a hollow ground edge behind it, and so forth. The world of ideas is always at your disposal when going the custom route.

CARRYING & ACCESSING

The last critical element we will discuss is how you carry and access the knife.

With a folding knife the obvious challenge lies in quickly getting it out and opened into your desired grip. This can be further compounded if you are blindsided by an Opponent, on the floor wrestling around, stuck in the Flailing of the Arms, or having to manage any Goal of the Process. A fixed blade with a properly made sheath and mounting system does offer more versatility in where you can carry your knife as well as faster and safer accessing options as it bypasses the extra opening step that the folder has. You could even carry a fixed blade in a pocket with a custom-made pocket sheath if it was necessary.

Any good sheath and mounting option has to have the following three features:

1. It needs to offer secure positive retention of the knife,

2. It needs to be comfortable to wear all day,

3. And it needs to be consistent in its accessibility.

The biggest drawback of knives which are worn around the neck in "neck sheaths" is that they move around, even if you could get access to it under your shirt in a hurry, you are never guaranteed it will be where you think it is. Again, this is compounded even further if you end up on the ground. Lastly, it is very difficult to access a neck knife covertly, especially when initiative has been lost. A good kydex sheath mounted on or anchored to your belt is the most secure method of carrying. Whether it's inside the waistband (IWB) or outside the waistband (OWB) is only relevant to you.

The positioning of the knife should ideally be in a place where it can be accessed with both hands, even if you're on your back.

The biggest challenge for people new to carrying a knife for defensive purposes however is their daily dress. For some people who work in more formal or corporate environments it can be tricky. Ladies in particular struggle with finding ways to carry a knife that are secure and accessible while still conforming to a dress code they feel comfortable in.

Sometimes you need to make some priority adjustments and decide what is more important to you. Other times it's possible to learn how to dress around the knife. If you have come this far though, you need to give it some serious thought and understand that the knife is simply no use to you if you can't get to it.

PIKAL KNIFE CONSIDERATIONS

The Pikal knife has gained quite a lot of popularity in the communities associated with defensive knife work, especially in the last 10 years or so, and as a result the options available to us for these kinds of knives are now wider than ever before. They are readily available through many custom knife makers and even some factory-made options.

This rise in popularity does come with some potential issues though, as many makers rally to create designs which allow them to stand out from the rest, certain key aspects which are important get overlooked or done away with all together. Unfortunately, in a day and age where information is freely available, and everyone feels entitled to follow their dreams, I am finding that all knife makers don't even necessarily understand the knife or its application anymore.

We have covered the more general rules to look out for when selecting an edged weapon, however when it comes to a Pikal or reverse edge, edge in knives specifically, there are some details you want to ensure are there.

NEUTRAL POINT INDEX

You will want to avoid blades that have a very extreme curve to them. The ideal Pikal blade has a point that, when held with your wrist in a natural, neutral position (no extension or contraction), aligns with the knuckles on your hand. In other words you want the point of the blade to align roughly with the centre of your hammer-fist.

The reason for this is that it becomes a natural aim point for you. Under duress, you do not want to have to think about where the point of your blade is in relation to how extended or contracted your wrist is. It's one less thing to have to mentally focus on in a situation that is already extremely mentally draining.

The blade can have a slight inward curve, and this can actually be quite beneficial to the cut, but the point should ideally be neutral.

LENGTH

Longer isn't always better. When specifically looking at Pikal blades the length of the blade in relation to the handle is important. The moment the blade becomes longer than the handle the laws of physics are no longer in your favor and the blade becomes a lever.

Outside the sterile environment of the training studio, blades can snag on clothing, get twisted up, bind, or even simply get stuck in bone or joint folds. If the blade is longer than the handle on your knife, the moment that happens, any force enacted on the blade is transferred to your hand, and subsequently your grip. A shorter blade transfers less leverage, and a blade which is shorter than the handle transfers almost nothing at all – in fact the leverage now works *in* your favor.

This leverage is one of the benefits of working a properly designed Pikal knife, and opens up all sorts of opportunities to manipulate an opponent, even into take-downs.

IMPROVISED WEAPON CONSIDERATIONS

We have already mentioned how The Maul can be interchanged with other weapons or objects and still remain an effective. When using an improvised weapon however, there are a couple of factors to keep in mind.

Always ask of the intended weapon: What will it actually do? This is something you should seriously train yourself to think of. Practice looking around you in any given environment, your kitchen, living room, your office at work, a shop you walk into, etc. Look at objects and begin to critically assess them in a couple of seconds to determine how you would most effectively use it if you had to.

It may sound self-explanatory to some, but for others this is an area you may need to really focus on, and that's ok.

There are 3 basic functions you can assign to improvised weapons, namely: bashing, poking or scraping.

If we were talking about purpose made edge and point tools, we would refer to these functions as: Chopping (bashing), stabbing (poking) and cutting/slashing (scraping). But the first thing we need to understand about improvised weapons is they are not ideal, and so our expectations of them need to be downgraded to base functions. Sometimes an object may have one of these functions, or sometimes two, so it's important to keep that in mind as well.

4. **Bashing**. Bashing is the base form of chopping. It's assigned to heavier objects that can be used to add mass to a strike and it won't necessarily cause any penetrative injuries, but more blunt force. Things like rocks or stones, heavy tools, bats and clubs, a coffee mug, a flashlight, even a smartphone in a rigid case... anything hard and with some heft to it.

5. **Poking**. Poking is the base form of stabbing. It's assigned to objects that have a point on them but are not necessarily going to be able to stab deeply, or are ergonomically not suitable for the job. Things like pens (even with a cap on), chopsticks, scissors, a stick, a snapped plastic ruler... anything that has even a moderate point to it and can be gripped firmly.

6. **Scraping.** Scraping is the base form of cutting. It's assigned to objects that have a slight edge to them but aren't necessarily designed to actually cut. These objects include keys, a money clip, certain types of jewelry*, bottle openers, small sticks, certain caps and lids, cigarette lighters... anything with a slightly hard edge that can be used in a proper grip.

It's worth noting that some jewelry can be used as an improvised weapon, but only if it doesn't harm you in the process. Finger rings with large protrusions may seem like an ideal improvised weapon, but if it gets snagged it can end up causing a severe injury to you, de-gloving or even breaking your finger.

TARGETING

With any improvised weapon the idea is not to prolong the fight. These kinds of weapons are generally good at surprising an Opponent and causing a moderate to severe amount of pain, with a few exceptions that can cause damage. In general, it's a good idea to limit your use of improvised weapons as a means to escape rather than a means to finish a fight. This is of course going to also be influenced by exactly what the circumstances are.

In any case, we advise using scrapers to mostly target the face, eyes and throat of an Opponent. Pokers can be used anywhere where there is hard tissue under the skin. These areas are most likely to generate a big pain response and cause the most Disruption, thus buying the most amount of time for you to create an opportunity.

A NOTE ABOUT NON-METALLIC WEAPONS

For the last few years there has been an increasing trend on non-metallic weapons in the self defense and combatives community. These are tools which are usually made from G10 material, carbon fiber, or recently, spikes made from antler or horn.

What we are going to say next might offend some seasoned readers, but it needs to be said. We do not consider these as "improvised weapons" because the intention is usually quite obvious to anyone with some training. Improvised weapons should be easily found or crafted and not resemble traditional weapons. We aren't saying the above mentioned non-metallic weapon types aren't effective, simply that carrying them isn't always as low-key as some people like to believe they are. As such, we simply don't refer to them as improvised weapons. Our rule of thumb is that if the object cannot pass direct scrutiny by a well trained security guard at a high security area then it's not really "improvised".

The only time the tools mentioned above should be seriously considered is when travelling through or intending on going into places where carrying weapons is prohibited. The goal with the tools mentioned above is in getting the weapon into the place, not in having an "improvised weapon" available. Obviously, while a non-metallic knife won't set off a metal detector, by carrying it in you might still be in contravention of the law – and subsequently if found you might not be allowed in, it might get confiscated, or you might even be arrested. Depending on context you might also have given grounds to the other party to either injure or kill you. If you don't know what you're doing here, then don't be stupid. While we fully believe in the use of weapons in self defense it doesn't really make a lot of sense to risk jail time for a perceived need or cool factor, especially when you understand that there are many more legal ways to ensure you have a usable tool for defensive application on you just about anywhere you go.

A really sturdy, good quality metal pen (not one of those overt "tactical" pens) is actually a really good investment. Shop around for one that is well made, classy, and feels good in a reverse hammer grip and you'll have a weapon as well as a really nice pen. With the exception of perhaps visiting a prison, you'll probably be allowed to take it with you just about anywhere you go.

If your "NPE Tool" requires you to be in fancy dress or explain its existence, then it's probably not as effective as you think it is at being low key.

Where things like G10 knives actually excel is in the fact that they weigh almost nothing, won't rust, and are generally pretty inexpensive. If you need something for jogging, or for the beach that won't require a belt to carry, and you won't be too worried about getting it wet, then a G10 knife is a great solution.

TRAINING WEAPONS & EQUIPMENT

As important as the knife you buy and carry, is the training weapons and equipment that you invest in. This book and the knife mean nothing if you don't put in any training and practice.

If you plan to seriously practice and carry a specific type of knife, then it's pretty much imperative that you also invest in a "trainer" for that specific type of knife. A trainer is what we call an inert or blunt version of the knife that is safe for training with. The point is rounded and there is no edge so it cannot lacerate or stab, but in terms of size, and ergonomics its identical to the live blade.

This kind of Trainer is sometimes called a "steel trainer" because the blade is also made of steel, but the metal it's made of is unimportant. What is important is that it's a hard trainer that has the same handle shape, same handle material and is sheathed and mounted in the same way as your live knife. You want it to be as close to the real knife as possible, including the weight.

One primary benefit of a hard trainer is that it can be worn and accessed the same way as your real knife. This is a really big benefit for training because it means you can train realistically and force yourself to access your weapon under duress, matching all the movement and complications that may arise if the scenario were real. The other primary benefit is that the hard trainer can be used operationally as a less than lethal control tool.

Remember, we learn from experience and ideally we want all movement to reside in System 1. The point of training is to create an experience as close to real as possible so that any complications happen in the training environment and can be overcome and worked through safely, as opposed to happening for real. A hard trainer is really the only medium that allows you to do this safely.

Obviously hard trainers are hard and it hurts when getting worked on by one. This should be seen as positive though. The pain response of being hit by a hard trainer in training is real and gives you a healthy respect for your Opponent's blade, and vice versa. The hard blade also doesn't yield which means you learn how leverage plays a role, and you experience how snagging, catching and twisting can happen in a fight, especially during the *flailing of the arms* and the Control phase.

One downside to using hard trainers is that light injuries become part of training. Bruises and scrapes are going to happen. This can be difficult for some students to deal with, not just from a physical pain perspective, but also an emotional one. There's nothing as demotivating as taking your shirt off to shower after training to visually see all the holes that would be in you if what you had just done had been for real. For some it has a way of forcing you to question whether this is something you'll ever be good at, which can be very demoralising. Just relax and continue training.

The other downside is it doesn't accurately simulate certain aspects of edged weapon encounters we know to be true. It's a fact that most people who have been stabbed do not feel anything and continue fighting until either the biomechanical or physiological effects start becoming apparent. With a hard trainer you will feel every stab and you will react unless you are very good at overriding your pain response. This is something we can work on by slow sparring. Slow speed allows you to better control the amount of pain you're inflicting on your sparring partner – enough to let them know they have been stabbed but not so much that they can't deal with it. Soft training knives do exist. Commercially they are typically made of rubber, and sometimes they are also made of EVA or foam. The benefits of a soft trainer are that you can hammer away at your training partner with very little physical damage. This is good for things like aggression training or perhaps for full speed scenario training, where the attacker may have a soft trainer so they can stab at full speed without hurting the student. Note here it should be a truly soft trainer.

Certain plastic or rubber trainers are also quite hard. The downside to these soft training knives is that they rarely resemble the real thing and cannot be sheathed or accessed like a real one. They do also lack the psychological element, there's no "oh that would have been bad if it were real" moments with soft trainers.

Pain in training can be really jarring for new students but once they get over that initial bit of shock and treat it like the learning experience that it is, hard trainers teach you a lot more.

If you really want to put the elements of The Maul into practice, a hard trainer and sheath is essential. The only other piece of equipment we recommend is a pair of safety glasses for you and your partner and a healthy respect for one another. Remember causing pain to your partner is ok, causing injury isn't. You should respect the fact that your partner allows you to do this to them.

OTHER EQUIPMENT

A strike board is a piece of wood you can mount on a wall. This will allow you to practice your accessing and stabbing at a specific target marked on the board. The outcome for this kind of training is to hone your accuracy and quickness. Try marking the board with numbers, and with each repetition choosing a number, accessing and stabbing.

If you have the money, a martial arts dummy is perfect for this kind of training as well and gives you a much more anatomically correct target.

THE MAUL

PART FIVE – EXTRAS

THE MAUL

170

CHAPTER FIFTEEN: STUPID THINGS PEOPLE SAY

We considered calling this chapter "let's see how many readers we can offend in one chapter," but decided against it as that's honestly not our intention. Have an open mind. And if you disagree - that's your right. If you want to argue though bring a sensible argument, based on research, fact, and consistently controlled for, experience. Alternatively arrange to meet the authors and show them.

"I would rather be judged by 12 than carried by 6."

Schalk:

Neither is necessary. Good Tactics will save you from the 12, accurate training will save you from the 6.

"Most dangerous knife in the world."

Gavin:

As a professional knife maker I have seen this statement more times than I care to remember. I can categorically state that there is no such thing as the "most dangerous knife in the world". They're all dangerous, even more so if used by skilled hands.

There is a big difference however between improvised, purpose made and adapted. A sharpened stick is just as lethal as a $2 000.00 custom knife, but it's probably not as nice to hold, EDC, work with, or look at.

This statement is 9 times out of 10 being applied to cheap, disposable knives that criminals would use (yes, I'm talking about Okapis). Cheap disposable knives, because they are churned out by the thousands, are often used in criminal attacks NOT because they are better, but because they are available. While these cheap knives no doubt have lethal potential it does not automatically mean they are good knives.

I quite often make the analogy to cars. You can buy a real cheap, 20 year old car that will get you from A to B. But you'll be able to make that trip a lot faster, more comfortably, more efficiently and probably with a lot less hassle in a newer, more expensive car. Well, it's the same when it comes to defensive knives…

And if you want to measure a knife's lethality based purely on body count, I think I'm right in saying the machete is the most dangerous knife in the world. Ask any Rwandan.

"Dull Edges are more dangerous than sharp edges."

Gavin:

No. They aren't. And by the way, this statement comes from a completely different context.

When I was 17 I started training to become a chef. One of the things my head chef told me was that a "Dull knife is more dangerous than a sharp one". In that specific context it makes sense. A dull knife will slip off the produce you're trying to cut, and then inevitably cut you. So, yes in that sense it's more dangerous.

But when it comes to defensive knives, no it's not. You want a sharp tool.

"If you know, you know."

Schalk:

The idea of esoteric knowledge, meaning knowledge known and knowable only by a select group, has been with us since ancient times. It's not a new concept. But recently it's become all the rage in the self defense and combatives industry. Whilst it creates a sense of community in those that actually do share certain types of experience, it also feeds the ego of the insecure and of those that don't actually have the experience.

Furthermore, to the regular person, the training enthusiast, the individuals honestly trying to improve themselves for life and operations, it creates an unnecessary sense of exclusion. That might be great for some, by all means if you need to do this to build your community go for it. But for ourselves (the authors), as individuals that honestly want to assist those around us, it's simply not our style. If you don't know ask. If we need to clarify anything for you we'll do so. If you need training we'll tell you. If your training is with us we'll quote and bill you accordingly.

"Criminals have better lawyers."

Schalk:

This is nonsense and probably comes from watching too many crime thrillers where the criminals are high level gang or mob members. In reality, realistic odds are the person mugging you or paid to kill you is going to be doing so for less money than most of us take home in a week.

Gavin:

Most criminals have public defenders, who don't cost anything.

"The law protects criminals."

Schalk:

No. The law just runs both ways. The same rights, and corresponding laws, that put the criminal in jail for killing someone, are what keep me out of jail for defending myself. Just as the criminal does not have the right to simply murder another person, I don't have the right to simply do so. Most people just don't like the legal system or are uneducated about how it works. If that's you, get over your dislike and/or educate yourself. There's much good work on this topic. A good place to start would be anything written by Marc MacYoung.

"Karambits."

Schalk:

The movement patterns required to run it well are simply too different from the bulk of other regular and improvised weapons available. This doesn't mean it's not effective as a weapon. To me it just feels like I would need to waste a lot of time learning to use the blade. Time which I feel could be better used elsewhere. Also, some of them are much too colourful for me.

Gavin:

I'll make you one if you want, but don't complain to me when you dissect your nipple the first time you try to flick it like Doug Marcaida.

"A failed assault will become a duel."

Gavin:

It's your job to not let it become a duel. If a failed assault becomes a duel then you aren't doing what you need to do to stop the attack.

Schalk:

Or he might just run away. Or it might be that you won - which is also a failed assault for the Opponent. Just saying.

"He really calls it like it is."

Schalk:

First of all, this presupposes that the acknowledging party already has an accurate picture of whatever "it" is. But seeing as we can't really test that let's move one. This seemingly important statement is pretty much devoid of content from which to judge its accuracy. Why not rather explain why you agree with the statement's subject in such a way that the reader can judge for themselves whether both parties are actually accurate? If you had the depth of knowledge and experience you should rightly be able to do so. It's a meaningless statement that frequently just gets abused to create association.

"Wrapped knife handles will soak in blood and DNA."

Gavin:

Not always. But the issue at hand is actually the context of the weapon's use. If you're concerned with your defensive knife holding blood and DNA evidence that will be used against you in trial later, then we are going to suggest that you rather spend more time understanding your laws governing use of lethal force than you spend worrying about DNA on your knife. Working within the bounds of the law, barring a few specific contexts and geographical locations, is actually both in your best interest as well as extremely do-able.

There seems to be a big disconnect sometimes with what people actually need to do within a self defense context, and what they fantasize about doing.

"Criminals are masters of the blade."

Schalk:

This is probably one of the most idiotic generalized statements ever to catch momentum in our industry. I say generalized in the sense that yes, granted, there will be good weapon handlers in the criminal environment, but that by no means indicates that all criminals are master weapon handlers.

The issue at hand relates to willingness vs. ability to use weapons or to fight. I'm sure in most readers' youth there was at least one guy that was known as a good fighter. He was always fighting. And as such, he was seen as a good fighter. In all honesty, he might have been somewhat good; all those fights might have built up some experience and taught him some lessons. But most probably, he was simply willing to fight. For those individuals that weren't that willing to fight, and possibly even feared this guy, it would be easy to confuse willingness with ability. Many criminals are willing to use weapons, more willing than the average law abiding citizen. But this doesn't mean that they have good, or even any for that matter, ability. Don't confuse the two. Barring Murphy's rule that anything that can go wrong might do so: put a well trained Mike Tyson up against the average willing bar room brawler and the odds are that Mike would take him down. For that matter, take an adult Mike Tyson starting his professional career vs. a Mike Tyson after three years of professional coaching. Who do you favor odds wise? Referring back to the example earlier in the book, and barring Murphy's rule again, put a gun wielding robber in a building with a well trained SWAT officer and the odds are it's the SWAT officer walking out of there.

Trainees need to have at least the same level of willingness as criminals, but they have the unique opportunity to find and invest in top quality training and practice. Most criminals are just willing, yes that makes them dangerous, but not masterful. This idea has especially gained traction in the systems which glorify gangsterism.

"Train with intent, not content."

Gavin:

I don't even know what this means.

Schalk:

Maybe YouTube content?

WHERE TO FROM HERE

Now that you have completed reading 'The Maul' we would like to invite you to join the community of other readers.

We have created three distinct groups which you can join and interact with.

Wider Community:

Please consider following our Facebook and Instagram pages

Book Readers Group:

For those who have read 'The Maul' and wish to discuss the concepts in it with other readers, practitioners and the authors. Please feel welcome to bring up any topics you are getting stuck on or need help with in this private Facebook Group.

The group is private and exclusively for those who have read the book and your purchase will need to be verified to gain approval.

Practitioners Patreon Tier:

If you want to delve deeper into understanding some of the techniques, concepts and training methodology in 'The Maul' you can subscribe to our Patreon Channel. Here we will upload instructional video content on a weekly basis. If there is something you need help with please reach out to us and we will do our best to explain or demonstrate it in video for you.

GLOSSARY

- **Assess** - From both the ARM Yourself protocol as well as the CCI Resolution Process. The continuous action of assessing PINs, TDs and Threat Indicators. Any other use of this word will not be capitalized.

- **Base Targets** - Injuries or disruptions which will affect the balance of an Opponent.

- **Chaos Drills** - A set of micro drills specifically selected and/or developed to increase performance in System 1. System 1 is a mode of functioning of the brain under certain conditions.

- **Close Combat Incident (CCI)** - An incident that occurs within arm's length, and that requires a combative application of force to resolve. It may be defensive or offensive in nature. In the context of this book it will primarily relate to hand to hand combat or the use of short length edged or pointed weapons.

- **Continuous Assessment** - The mental discipline of continuously assessing various factors in the CCI whilst the CCI is still active. Continuous Assessment does not come instinctively and should be trained.

- **Control** - Neutralizing the immediate threat through controlling its movement. A moment of stabilization of the chaos of the CCI in order to transition to a Takedown. Takedown. The act of putting the Opponent on the floor. Finish. The final action taken to reach the desired outcome in terms of resolving the CCI. Determined by the context of the situation as well as the primary outcome of the Trainee.

- **Correct Execution** - Correct Execution should be defined BOTH by an accurate movement pattern as well as successful application in an Unscripted Training or Play Learning environment. Correct Execution does not mean a person can simply successfully mimic what a movement pattern looks like, it means that they can use the movement pattern effectively and also achieve its intended outcome. This is the reason that Correct Execution can only be measured in terms of performance in Unscripted Training or Play Learning environments.

- **Current Reality (CR)** - The situation, as well as all its factors present, at the current moment in time.

- **Disrupt** - The act of applying force to an Opponent with the goal of gaining their compliance in transitioning to a following Goal. Entry. A technique used to close range.

- **Dive Entry** - The Maul's primary Entry technique. Essentially the evolutionary flinch reaction that has been refined and adapted to increase its effectivity and vary its application. It is a robust technique used both offensively and defensively, and very early in the CCI Process. Primarily used to close range and either to stop the attack immediately or to setup a transition into Control.

- **Drop Step** - A controlled fall using gravity to accelerate body movement, placing as much mass, at as high an acceleration possible, behind a strike.

- **Flow Drill / Flowing** - The main movement patterns of The Maul taught and developed in a single drill.

- **Four Main Lines** - The four main lines of movement used in The Maul's attacks. Includes Lines 1 to 4 individually.

- **Fundamentals and Skills, Techniques, Tactics, Procedures and Outcomes** - The primary matrix used to refine and select training components. Outcomes determine Procedures and Techniques required. Tactics explain how to use Techniques and Procedures to achieve certain outcomes. Procedures are multiple Techniques strung together. Techniques contain specific Skills and Fundamentals.

- **Goal / Goals** - The CCI Resolution or Maul Process Goals specifically. Any other use of this word will not be capitalized.

- **Move** - From the ARM Yourself protocol. The action taken in response to the Trigger set. Any action falls into one of the following four categories: Subvert, Escape, Defend and Mitigate. Context will determine the rules and outcomes of Defend.

- **Nature of Violence / the Nature** - Violence is inherently complex, extremely dynamic, and therefore has an unpredictable outcome.
- **Opponent** - As above, the Opponent is a catchall term for any person or persons opposing the Trainee, whether inside or outside the training environment.

- **Pre-Incident iNdicators (PINs)** - A wide range of indicators that can be learned which assist us to Assess and develop our Situational Awareness. There is a lot of good material available concerning PINs, and seeing as it is not the focus of this book, we gladly refer you elsewhere. In our opinion the training from The CP Journal group is leading the way here.

- **Pikal** - A type of combative knife specifically designed to be held in reverse grip (tip down) with the primary cutting edge facing inward (toward the user). Referred to in this book as "Pikal" or "Pikal Knife.

- **Play Learning** - Any training where there is no specific focus on a Technique or Procedure, neither is there a linear progression of the situation defined or expected. A very basic outcome and a starting position might be defined but the resolution of the CCI is left completely in the hands of the participants.

- **Process** - The CCI Resolution Process, or in the case of this book, The Maul Process. Any other use of this word will not be capitalized.

- **Ranging / Ranged** - A method for finding the perfect range for a Technique. Any other use of these words will not be capitalized.

- **Ready** - From the ARM Yourself protocol. The act of mentally priming oneself for action, or in ARM Yourself lingo, priming oneself to Move. Priming is accomplished by the setting of IF THIS THEN THAT Triggers. There are three main types of Triggers: Confirmation, Opportunity and Necessity Triggers.

- **Situational Awareness** - The ability to make accurate judgements concerning how an event is unfolding.

- **Switches** - Injuries or disruptions that have an immediate effect.

- **Switch / Switching** - The action of the brain moving from a System 1 to System 2 type functioning and vice versa.

- **Tactic Determinants (TDs)** - Any factor present that influences which tactic one should adopt. In the context of this book it might relate to issues of range, weapon hand, weapon type, injuries held by either the defender, operator or Opponent. Assessment TDs should happen continuously and influence the selection and application of techniques or procedures.

- **Tethering / Tethered / Tether** - A method of controlling the Opponent through positive pressure and without having to apply a strict joint lock.

- **The Four Ds** - Four different actions that the open arm can take to assist in the CCI. All four actions start with the letter D for ease of remembrance: Distract, Deflect, Disrupt and Disengage.

- **Threat Indicators** - Any attribute that is either a clear or highly probable indicator of someone or something being a threat. Meant as a shortcut in assessing. Examples being weapons, hands being purposefully hidden, highly dominant or uncomfortable behavior, expressions of intent to harm and so forth.

- **Threshold** - A set of correct conditions, which having been met, forces the Switch to occur.

- **Timers -** Injuries or disruptions which take time to have an effect.

- **Trainee** - Because this book was written specifically to provide value to a wide audience, we needed a collective term that would cover the audience. With the catchall term of Trainee we include student, client, team members, self defense enthusiast, civilian, martial artists, sport fighters, LEOs, operators, as well as anyone else that will be learning from the contents.

- **Triggers -** The qualifier, set mentally by the Trainee, which indicates the exact moment to Move.

- **Unscripted Training -** Any training where there is a specific Technique or

Procedure being practiced but not within or against a predetermined situation or attack.

- **Working Group** - A group of Trainees or Opponents working together at a given time. The group will consist of all participants, whether team, individual defender or operator, bystander or any other Opponents.

Made in the USA
Monee, IL
02 August 2020